D0793348

The Singing Top

World Folklore Advisory Board

Simon J. Bronner, Ph.D.
Distinguished Professor of Folklore and American Studies
Pennsylvania State University at Harrisburg

Joseph Bruchac, Ph.D.
Abenaki Storyteller and Writer

Natalie O. Kononenko, Ph.D.
Professor of Slavic Language and Literature
University of Virginia

Norma J. Livo, Ed.D.
Writer and Storyteller

Margaret Read MacDonald, Ph.D.
King County Library System

MacDonald, Margaret Read
The singing top : tales
from Malaysia, Singapore
2008.
33305213368815
gi   09/08/08

The Singing Top

Tales from Malaysia, Singapore, and Brunei

Retold and Edited by Margaret Read MacDonald

World Folklore Series

**LIBRARIES
U N L I M I T E D**

A Member of the Greenwood Publishing Group

Westport, Connecticut • London

Library of Congress Cataloging-in-Publication Data

MacDonald, Margaret Read, 1940-
 The singing top : tales from Malaysia, Singapore, and Brunei / retold and edited by Margaret Read MacDonald.
  p. cm. — (World folklore series)
 Includes bibliographical references and index.
 ISBN 978-1-59158-505-3 (alk. paper)
 1. Tales—Malaysia. 2. Tales—Singapore. 3. Tales—Brunei. I. Title.
GR315.M33   2008
398.209595—dc22   2008011520

British Library Cataloguing in Publication Data is available.

Copyright © 2008 by Margaret Read MacDonald

All rights reserved. No portion of this book may be reproduced, by any process or technique, without the express written consent of the publisher. Exceptions include reproduction and performance in educational, not-for-profit settings.

Library of Congress Catalog Card Number: 2008011520
ISBN: 978-1-59158-505-3

First published in 2008

Libraries Unlimited, 88 Post Road West, Westport, CT 06881
A Member of the Greenwood Publishing Group, Inc.
www.lu.com

Printed in the United States of America

The paper used in this book complies with the Permanent Paper Standard issued by the National Information Standards Organization (Z39.48–1984).

10   9   8   7   6   5   4   3   2   1

CONTENTS

Part 3: Tales from the Ethnic Peoples of Borneo

Part 4: Proverbs and Pantun

Part 5: Malay Children's Songs and Games

ACKNOWLEDGMENTS

I have had the good fortune to be involved in several books in the World Folklore Series produced by Libraries Unlimited. I encouraged friends to pull together collections of folktales from their countries, and I helped by editing and annotating their books. Supaporn Vathanaprida contributed *Thai Tales*; Murti Bunanta compiled *Indonesian Folktales*; the Rio storyteller Livia de Almeida prepared *Brazilian Folktales*; the Cuban teller Livia Pérez created *From the Winds of Manguito: Desde los vientos de Manguito*, with translation help from the Argentinian teller Paula Martín; and the Lao scholar and storyteller Wajuppa Tossa worked with Kongdeuane Nettavong to produce *Lao Folktales*.

This collection of tales from Malaysia, Brunei, and Singapore however, draws from friends and travels so disparate that I chose to prepare this collection myself, with considerable help from friends in several locales.

I first began telling Malay tales in 1969 when I was employed as a storyteller by the Singapore American School. My Singapore friends, Chee Keng Soon and Chee Keuk Fong, immediately plied me with tales of the little mouse deer trickster, Kancil/Kantjil/Kantchil, sometimes called Pelandok. Kancil's antics remain a favorite of Singapore and Malaysian children. Thanks to the Chees for introducing me to the wonderful folk culture of Malaysia and Singapore.

More recently, I have been involved with the excellent Southeast Asian storytelling festivals produced in Singapore. There I met contemporary storytellers who are sharing tales from Singapore's many cultures. Kiran Shah, Sheila Wee, Kamini Ramachandran, Rosemarie Somaiah, Roger Jenkins, and Panna Kantilal have shared tales and knowledge with me. I am especially grateful to Sheila, Kiran, and Kamini for a fun afternoon singing Malay children's songs!

Through several years of offering storytelling workshops in Malaysia, I have met wonderful folks who were eager to share their own culture. Mohammed Taib Mohammed of the Perak State Library and Ipoh children's librarian Suraya Ariffin have been especially helpful in introducing me to Malay culture.

At a library conference in Kuala Lumpur I met librarians from the distant states of Sabah and Sarawak, located on the island of Borneo. They invited me to offer storytelling workshops for their librarians. And so I was introduced to another facet of the folklore of this region, the amazing tales of the various ethnic groups of Borneo. In Sabah, Kadazan librarians shared delightful stories. Arrangements were made for me to stay overnight in a Sungai village and hear traditional tellers. In both Sabah and Sarawak I found that the museums had published folktale collections drawn from their several ethnic peoples.

I need to thank especially Mary Catharine Golangai, of the Sabah State Library, who so lovingly shared her culture with me. And enormous thanks are due to librarian Yunis Rojiin. One day in 2003, as we were returning from a long day of storytelling in rural areas, Yunis said, "You know, your stories remind me of things my grandmother used to tell me." "What things, Yunis?" And she began to tell long, amazing tales that her grandmother had told her as a child. I grabbed my pencil and paper and began to write as fast as I could. Meanwhile my son-in-law, Nat Whitman, grabbed a pencil and began to notate the music in the refrains Yunis was singing. We got it all down and were able to present Yunis with a copy for correction the next day. On my next visit, in 2005, Yunis sat down and told me many more tales she remembered from her grandmother.

Joanna Kissey arranged a homestay for my family in Kampong Batu Putih, where we were fortunate to hear Abdul Rahman Bulinti Lindas and his sister share an evening of Sungai tales. We were especially lucky that a Malay-speaking woman from Kota Kinabalu was visiting that night. Our host translated the tales into Malay, and the Malay speaker translated them into English for us.

These tales were not collected in any scholarly way; they were just tales I bumped into, which are too good to keep to myself. The tellers all asked that their stories be passed on. So I share them in this collection.

INTRODUCTION

This book presents tales from the Malay people and from some of the indigenous people of Malaysia. The Malay culture is found both in Peninsular Malaysia and along the coasts of the island of Borneo, where lie the Malaysian states of Sabah and Sarawak and the tiny country of Brunei. Although the population of Malaysia is almost a quarter Chinese and 7 percent Indian, this collection cannot attempt to include the folklore of those cultures. Several indigenous peoples reside in the interior of the Malay peninsula, but their stories do not appear in this book. The book is confined to tales of the Malay people and those of certain indigenous peoples of Malaysia. In 2007 the Malay made up 50 percent of the population of Malaysia; indigenous peoples constituted 11 percent of the population.

The area of the ancient Malay culture extended across much of Indonesia as well, so some of the tales here take place in Sumatra and Java, as well as on the peninsula.

Malay folklore includes animal tales, such as those of Kantchil the Mousedeer, tales of local heroes, legends of specific locales, and complicated epics combining historical fact with fanciful episodes. Malay folk literature includes material retold from Indian tradition, such as stories from the *Panchatantra* and the *Ramayana* and *Mahabharata* epics. Because these tales are available elsewhere, I have not included them here. Malay folk literature also includes much material from Islamic tradition. These legends tend to be lengthy and deserve a book of their own. So here, for the most part, are only those tales specific to the Malay people.

In this collection I also include tales of the indigenous peoples of Saba, Sarawak, and the country of Brunei. I am fortunate to present here for the first time in English the extraordinary tales of Gunih Rampasan, grandmother of Sabah State Library storyteller Yunis Rojiin Gabu.

Singapore is physically and in some ways culturally a part of this region. It appears in many of the Malay legends. There is an active contemporary storytelling scene in Singapore, and I have included some of the favorite tales of those tellers. You will find tales here from Jessie Goh, Panna Kantilal, Kamini Ramachandran, Rosemary Somaiah, Kiran Shah, and Sheila Wee.

So we have here a fascinating selection of tales. Part 1 introduces the countries of the tales' origins. The first five tales in Part 2 delve into the amazing magical and historical legends of Malaya. They are followed by tales about the trickster figure Kantchil the Mouse Deer, plant fables, and one of the Malay fools, Pak Pandir. In Part 3 we cross the seas to

Borneo and enter a totally different world, tales of the Kadazandusun, Sungai, and Dyak peoples. Part 4 contains a selection of Malay and Dusun proverbs and Malay pantun (a poetic form). We then take time to enjoy some Malay songs and games in Part 5.

Unless otherwise noted, all tales are retold by this author. A glossary, scholarly notes about the tales' origins, and a bibliography to lead you to more books of Malaysian tales appear at the end of the book.

MAP OF MALAYSIA, SINGAPORE, AND BRUNEI

Island of
Borneo

Brunei   Sabah (Malaysia)

Sarawak
(Malaysia)

Kalimantan
(Indonesia)

PART 1

The Countries from Which
These Stories Come

ABOUT MALAYSIA

Where Is Malaysia?

Malaysia is a country with two separate geographic sites. If you look at a map of Southeast Asia you will see a long peninsula hanging down from Thailand into the ocean. The top part of this peninsula is inhabited by Thai people. The bottom part is inhabited by Malay. Where the two join lies a confusing land in which Thai and Malay share space, sometimes uneasily. The part of Malaysia that lies on the peninsula is referred to as Peninsular Malaysia. Here is the capital of Malaysia, Kuala Lumpur. Far away across the South China Sea lies the island of Borneo. On this island are two states, Sabah and Sarawak, which are also part of the present-day political entity Malaysia. The distance from the capital of Sabah, Kota Kinabalu, to Kuala Lumpur is over 1,000 miles across the sea!

How did a country end up with such far-apart pieces? The Malay people were a seagoing people, and they traveled throughout the South China Sea. They settled in the lower part of the Malay peninsula and also along the shores of the many islands that stretch from Singapore to the Philippines. Anthropologists speak of the entire area, including the islands of present-day Indonesia, as the Malay Archipelago. However, many different cultures and dialects exist in these islands.

In the nineteenth century, the British became a ruling force in Peninsular Malaysia, which was at that time called Malaya. The British also had a strong presence in the countries of Sarawak and Sabah, located on the northern half of the island of Borneo. The peoples of the interior of Borneo are indigenous peoples, although many Malay live in the seaside areas of Sarawak and Sabah. When the British withdrew from Malaya, they also withdrew from Sarawak, Sabah, and Singapore. It was decided that Malaya, Sarawak, Sabah, and Singapore would be joined in a new state called Malaysia. Soon after, Singapore withdrew from the union and become an independent country.

The original country of Malaya was divided into nine Sultanates. Before the British took power, each was ruled by a hereditary Sultan. After independence was declared in 1957, certain powers were retained by those Sultans. Although the country is now ruled by an elected government, the Sultans are still important cultural figures. One Sultan is considered the head of state, and this position rotates among the nine Sultanates every five years.

Penang and Melaka, also states in Malaya, did not have Sultanates and therefore do not take part in this rotation; nor do Sabah and Sarawak.

Colonization and Cultural Cross-Fertilization

Historically, Malaya was situated in a very important position for shipping and trade. Ships from India, China, and eventually Europe all made their way through the Straits of Malacca, a seaway that lies between the peninsula and the island of Sumatera. From the seventh to eleventh centuries the Malay kingdom of Kedah, along with Palembang on Sumatera, formed the heart of the Srivajaya kingdom, which controlled the Straits of Malacca. But in the eleventh century the Chola Empire of South India attacked Kedah and destroyed it. By the fourteenth century a Malay–Hindu kingdom, Majapahit, based on Java, controlled the Malay Archipelago. The influence of Indian culture is still evident in Malaysian arts.

From the opposite direction came Chinese ships, passing through the Straits of Malacca en route to India to trade. By the fifteenth century the Chinese ships were also making regular calls at Malacca. Thus, Singapore, Malacca, and Penang all developed large colonies of Chinese immigrants. Over time these Chinese intermarried with Malay women and adopted Malay customs and language. They form a special group now called the Peranakan Chinese.

Also by the fifteenth century, a new religion had taken hold in Mallaca: Islam had arrived from the Middle East. In 1414 Prince Parameswara of Mallaca converted to Islam, changed his name to Megat Iskandar Shah, and took the title of Sultan. Mallaca began to grow in power, crowding out the Majapahit Empire with its Indian influence. Islam, with its own new culture, spread throughout the region.

The trade winds blew ships from both directions directly to Malacca, so that the north monsoon in the spring brought Chinese junks, and the southwest monsoon brought Arabic and Indian ships.

By the sixteenth century, the important port of Malacca had drawn the attention of the Europeans. The Portuguese arrived in 1511 with eighteen ships and 1,400 men. But the Dutch also wanted Malacca. After years of battles beginning in 1597, the Dutch finally took Malacca from the Portuguese in 1641. The Dutch were mainly interested in controlling the trade routes, and they gave the Sultan free reign to rule the interior.

In 1795 the British arrived to rule Malacca. At the time, the Dutch were under French rule, so they let the British take over Malacca temporarily. In 1824, under the Colonial Treaty of London, the British took permanent control of Malacca. The British also took an interest in Penang and in Singapore, a sparsely inhabited island, on which they had established a colony in 1819.

By the middle of the nineteenth century, the British were colonizing the interior of the Malay peninsula. The Malay lived mainly on the coast and along rivers. In 1836 Malaya had an estimated 250,000 inhabitants. But beginning around 1820, a large influx of landless peasants from South China began to arrive in the Straits Settlements (Penang, Malacca, and

Singapore). They moved inland, working in tin mines, clearing forests, building towns and roads, and settling the interior. At the same time the British were taking increasing control of the country. At first the British acted as "advisors" to the Sultans. But gradually they usurped power.

In the last quarter of the nineteenth century the British began to bring Tamil workers from the south of India to Malaya. These people provided even cheaper labor than the Chinese and did not organize themselves into secret societies as the Chinese did. These workers built roads and railroads and filled a need for workers on the European-owned plantations.

In 1942, during World War II, the Japanese invaded Malaya, Singapore, and Borneo. British citizens were incarcerated in concentration camps; many died during forced marches through difficult terrain. After the war, the Malay states were still under British control, but a movement for independence soon began. Independence was declared on August 31, 1957. Soon after, Singapore joined the Federation of Malay States, and in the 1960s Sabah and Sarawak joined. In 1965 Singapore withdrew from the federation to form its own city-state.

Today's Malaysia

Today Malaysia consists of thirteen states: Perlis, Kedah, Penang, Kelantan, Selangor, Perak, Terengganu, Pahang, Negeri Sembilan, Johore, Melaka, Sabah, and Sarawak. There are also federal territories: the capital city, Kuala Lumpur; Putra Jaya (planned to become a new seat of government); and Labuan (an island off the coast of Sabah, which obtained separate status in 1984).

The ethnic Malay have the rights of *bumiputra*, sons of the soil. They are given special privileges, such as first rights to university entrance and advantages in land purchase and business ownership. Theoretically, other indigenous ethnic groups in Malaysia—such as the Orang Asli of the peninsula and the Kadazan, Dusun, Dyak and other ethnicities of Borneo—also have *bumiputra* rights.

Islam is the official religion of Malaysia, but religious freedom is guaranteed to other faiths. An ethnic Malay, however, is expected to adhere to the Islamic faith.

Malaysia's large exports include rubber, palm oil, timber, and electronic and manufactured products. Oil and gas exports are a major source of income.

According to the U.S. Department of State, in 2007 the population of Malaysia was 50.2 percent Malay, 24.5 percent Chinese, 11 percent indigenous, 7.2 percent Indian, 5.9 percent non-Malaysian citizens, and 1.2 percent other. The religions observed are Islam (60.4 percent), Buddhist (19.2 percent), Christian (9.1 percent), Hindu (6.3 percent), Confucian (2.6 percent), tribal (0.8 percent), other (0.4 percent), and none (1.2 percent).

SINGAPORE

The island of Singapore is located at the bottom tip of the Malay peninsula. It is separated from the peninsula of Malaya by only a channel of water, which is crossed easily by bridge.

At one time the city was an outpost of the Javan Srivijaya Empire and was called Temasek. But by the end of the fourteenth century Temasek had declined in importance. The island was under rule of the Sultan of Johore for several centuries, but in 1819 Sir Stamford Raffles signed a treaty with Sultan Husssein Shah to develop a trading post and settlement. The port founded there thrived and eventually took trade away from Malacca. The influx of Chinese emigrants to this port city soon created a majority Chinese population and culture. In 2006 the Singapore population was 75.2 percent Chinese, 13.6 percent Malay, 8.8 percent Indian, and 2.4 percent Eurasian.

Singapore has four official languages: English, Tamil, Malay, and Mandarin. The use of Mandarin Chinese is being promoted because this language has been adopted as the official form of Chinese by mainland China and Taiwan. Older Chinese still speak their own dialects: Cantonese, Hokkien, Hakka, Teochew, and Hainanese. Some people still speak the Baba Malay dialect of the Peranakan Chinese.

In 1959 Singapore became an independent state, with Lee Kuan Yew as prime minister. Singapore joined the Federation of Malay States in 1962, but withdrew in 1965 to pursue its course as an independent nation. During Lee Kuan Yew's years as prime minister the tiny nation became wealthy, with excellent social services for all of its residents. Lee retired in 1990. His son, Lee Hsien Loong, became prime minister in 2004.

BORNEO

The island of Borneo is the third largest island in the world. In addition to the states of Sarawak and Sabah, the island also includes the tiny country of Brunei.

Sabah

Sabah lies at the northern end of the island of Borneo. In 2006 the population was 6.5 percent Brunei Malay, 35.1 percent Kadazan/Dusun, 13.4 percent Bajau, 4.8 Murut, 14.2 percent Chinese, and 26 percent non-Malaysian citizens.

Sabah was at one time a part of the Sultanate of Brunei. In 1658 a large portion of northeast Borneo was given to the Sultan of Sulu as a gift. But in 1865 the same area was leased to the American consul at Brunei by the Sultan of Brunei. It gradually passed through various hands to the British North Borneo Company. In 1963 Britain handed back control of North Borneo and the country joined the Federation of Malaysia as one of its states, taking the name Sabah.

Sarawak

Following the coast back down the island of Borneo we come to the small Sultanate of Brunei, still an independent country, and then to the state of Sarawak. Sarawak joined the Federation of Malaysia in 1963. Sarawak had also been a part of the Sultanate of Brunei at one time, but in 1841 was granted by the Sultan of Brunei to James Brooke in thanks for his help in subduing the local inhabitants. Brooke, known as "The White Rajah," was later succeeded by his nephew and his nephew's son. The last "white rajah," Sir Charles Vyner Brooke, abdicated after World War II. The country was briefly a crown colony of Britain before achieving independence.

The 2004 census showed that 29 percent of Sarawak's population is Iban (a Dyak ethnic group), 25.6 percent is Chinese, 22.4 percent is Malay, 5.5 percent is Melanau, 8 percent is Bidayuh, 5.7 percent is other bumiputra, and 3.8 percent is of other backgrounds. Some of the state's many indigenous groups are the Bidayuh, Melanau, Kenyah, Kayan, Kedayan, Murut, Bisayah, Kelabit, Berawan, and Penan.

Brunei

Sandwiched between Sabah and Sarawak is the tiny country of Brunei. At one time the Sultan of Brunei ruled over much of Sabah and Sarawak. Today the country is small, but it remains an independent nation. The Sultan of Brunei is one of the richest men in the world! Brunei sits on vast oil reserves. Sultan Haji Hassanal Bolkiah is a descendant of a family that has ruled in Brunei since the fifteenth century. The country consists of two small pieces of land connected by sea, with a piece of Sarawakian land separating them inland.

The population of Brunei is 73.8 percent Malay, 14.8 percent Chinese, and 11.4 percent indigenous and other.

From all of these places—Peninsular Malaya, Singapore, Sabah, Sarawak, and Brunei—come amazing stories. Some of them are shared in this book.

PART 2

Tales of the Malay People

Legends of Malacca, Johore, and Singapore from the *Sedjaret Malayou*

   The legends in this section are retold from the *Sedjaret Malayou,* known also as *The Malay Anals.* This lengthy historical legend is filled with magical elements. It is said to have been begun on Sunday, May 13, 1612, while Sultan 'Ala'u-d-din Ri-ayat Shah of Johore was being held prisoner. It is said that he commissioned Tun Sri Lanang of the Royal Court of Johore to compile this history. There are, however, several versions of the manuscript, containing varying details. The manuscripts were set down in classical Malay in the Jawi script. A page of the manuscript can be seen online at http://www/sabrizain.org/malay/malays1.htm. An English version translated by M. Devic and Chauncey C. Starkweather can be read online at http://www.yorku.ca/inpar/sedjaret_devic.pdf.

A SHIP FULL OF RUSTY NEEDLES

How the Chinese Convinced Rajah Suran
to Sail Back to India

Retold by Singapore storyteller Sheila Wee

You will notice that the tales from the Sedjaret Malayou t*alk of visitors from India, China, and throughout Southeast Asia. The Malay peninsula was always a crossroads, encountering visitors from many lands.*

*O*nce in the time long ago, there was a king. His name was Rajah Suran, and he ruled over India. But India wasn't enough for him. He wanted to be the most powerful king in the world. He made all the princes of the nearby countries bow down to him, pay him taxes of rice and gold, and call him the most powerful king.

Still he wasn't happy. There was someone who refused to say that he was the most powerful, that he was the greatest king, and that was the Emperor of China.

This made Rajah Suran very angry, and he decided he would invade China. He gathered a huge army with soldiers from every part of his empire. The army was so big that it was impossible to count the number of soldiers. It was impossible to count the number of weapons. It was impossible to count the numbers of horses and elephants.

But Rajah Suran had a problem. You see, he wasn't exactly sure where China was. He thought that it was in the south, so he led his army into Myanmar (Burma) and followed the coast southward.

People said that wherever the army passed, the forests were flattened, the rivers dried up, and the mountains trembled. People said it took six months for that army to pass by a single village.

Down through Myanmar they went and into Thailand, then farther south into Malaysia. They kept on marching for month after month, until at last they reached the beaches of the Straits of Johor and stood looking across the water to the island of Singapore. Though in those long ago times it was not called Singapore; it was called Temasek.

There they had to stop and build rafts to ferry them across the water. This took some time, but at last the whole army was assembled on the north shore of Temasek. Rajah Suran gave the order to march southward, but it didn't take long before they reached the Southern Sea and could go no farther.

Rajah Suran realized that if he wanted to reach China he would now have to travel by sea. So he set his men to building hundreds of strong ships. But he still didn't know which way to go, so he also sent men off in every direction with instructions to find the way to China and find it quickly.

Now, Rajah Suran's journey to Temasek had not been a secret, could not be a secret, not with so many men, horses, and elephants making the ground thunder with their footsteps.

Traders who sailed the coast trading in gold, spices and aromatic wood heard of Rajah Suran's plan, and they told their friends about the huge army that was looking for the way to China. Now their friends told their friends and their friends told their friends and their friends told their friends, until eventually someone told the Emperor of China himself.

The Emperor was very worried. He called his ministers together and asked their advice. "What shall we do? If Rajah Suran finds the way to our land, he will surely defeat us; his army is so much bigger, so much stronger than ours. We must find a way to stop him."

The Emperor and his ministers sat down to think. They thought all day and they thought all night, and then just as the dawn was breaking, the Chief Minister burst out laughing.

"Oh yes, I have it, I have a very good plan," he cried. He whispered his plan into the Emperor's ears and the Emperor smiled for the first time in days.

"Yes, that is a very good plan; go and get the things you need at once."

And so the Chief Minister went down to the harbor to find a ship to sail to Temasek, to sail to Singapore. But he didn't look for the best ship, the fastest ship, the newest ship. No, he searched the harbor until he found the oldest ship there was. Its planks were worn and its sails were yellow with age.

The other ministers, who had not heard the plan, were very puzzled. They wondered how this old ship was going to help them, how it was going to stop Rajah Suran's mighty army.

They were even more puzzled when they heard who was going to sail the ship and what it was going to carry.

The Chief Minister chose the sailors himself. He chose the oldest men he could find. Some of them were so old they could hardly walk and had to be carried onto the ship.

"Old men, sailing an old ship; the Chief Minister's gone crazy," the people said.

Then the Chief Minister did something that seemed just as ridiculous: He ordered that huge fruit trees should be dug up, planted into pots, and carried on board the ship.

"Crazy, crazy, he must have gone crazy," the people said.

Last, he ordered that all the needles in the city should be brought to the palace. By the next morning the palace courtyard was filled with great piles of sewing needles.

The Chief Minister ordered the servants to pick out all the old and rusty needles and put them into sacks. The servants worked hard, and by nightfall they had gathered fifty sacks full of rusty needles.

One of them approached the minister. "We've gathered fifty sacks of rusty needles. Shall we throw them away?"

"Throw them away! No! Don't throw them away, put them on board the ship!"

The servants did as they were told, but they were sure that the Chief Minister and the Emperor had both gone crazy.

Everyone wondered, "An old ship with old sailors, old fruit trees, and old rusty needles; how is that going to save us from the terrible army of Rajah Suran?"

The Emperor and the Chief Minister heard what people were saying, but they did not say a word, they just smiled as they waved the ship off on its journey.

A few weeks later the ship arrived in Temasek. Rajah Suran and all his men were still there, and they still didn't know the way to China.

When the lookouts spotted the old ship limping into the harbor, with huge fruit trees growing on its deck and a crew of old grandfathers, they couldn't stop laughing. Soon everyone had heard about the strange ship, and even Rajah Suran himself came to take a look.

"Where have you come from?" he asked. "What country is it that has such old sailors?"

The oldest of the sailors spoke up, "We have come from China. When we set out we were all strong young men—we were carrying a cargo of fruit tree seeds and iron bars. But it took us so long to get here that we have grown old, the seeds have become trees, and the iron bars have rusted away to tiny needles." And he opened one of the sacks of needles to show Rajah Suran.

Rajah Suran looked down and sighed. If China was that far away , he would be an old man before they got there, and his soldiers would be old also—too old to fight. No, it was not worth it; he would send his army back to India and find some other, nearer land to conquer.

And so the huge army turned around and marched back the way it had come and China was saved.

But some stories say that Rajah Suran himself did not go straight back to India. They say that he followed a dream and went down below the waves of the Southern Sea, where he married the Princess Mahtab-al-Bhari, the Sea King's daughter. They say they had three sons and lived together happily for many years. But then Rajah Suran began to miss the world above the ocean, to miss the sunshine, the trees, and the birds flying free in the sky.

He became sadder and sadder until at last his wife told him that he should go back to his own land, back to his own people. He wanted to take her and their sons with him. But the great Sea King said no, his daughter and the boys must remain in the land below the sea. But he did promise that when the boys grew into men, they would come up out of the sea and become kings on the land.

And some people say that is just what happened; when the boys grew up they came out of the sea near a place called Palembang in Sumatra. And they did become kings. The youngest prince became the king of Palembang and was given the title Sangsapurba.

In time, Sangsapurba married and had a son. Now, if you were from Singapore you would have heard of that son before, for his name was Sang Nila Utama, the very same Sang Nila Utama who sailed across stormy waters to land in Temasek, saw what he thought was a lion, and gave our country its name, Singapura—the lion city. But that, as they say, is another story.

RAJAH SURAN DIVES BENEATH THE SEA

A Magical Tale

Here is a more lengthy telling of Rajah Suran's adventures under the sea, taken from the Sedjaret Malayou.

After Rajah Suran had decided to return home to India, he still wanted to do one final thing before he left Temasek (Singapore).

"The contents of the land are known to me," said Rajah Suran, "But how can I learn about the contents of the sea? I need to enter under the sea, to learn what is there."

So Rajah Suran ordered his skilled men to prepare a box of glass, with a lock and fastenings on the inside, so that he could shut himself into it. They fastened this marvelous glass box with a chain of pure gold and presented it to Rajah Suran. He was delighted and rewarded them richly for their work.

Then Rajah Suran shut himself into the box and had it lowered, lowered, lowered into the sea, until it rested on the sea bottom.

Now the glass box of the Rajah Suran landed in a land under the sea called Dika. There Rajah Suran opened the box and emerged. He found himself in a wonderful land. There was a fine town and a huge population there. The people called themselves the Badsam people. Some were believers (Muslim), and some were unbelievers.

The people were astounded at the appearance of Rajah Suran and took him to their king, who was called Agtab-al-Ard (Bowels of the Earth). King Agtab-al-Ard was amazed to meet Rajah Suran. "Where do you come from? Who are you?"

"I am from the world," replied Rajah Suran. "My name is Rajah Suran."

"Do you mean," gasped King Agtab-al-Ard, "that there is another world besides ours?"

"The world," replied Rajah Suran, "contains many peoples."

"Glory be to God Almighty!" said King Agtab-al-Ar. And he brought Rajah Suran to sit beside him on his throne.

Now Agtab-al-Ar had a beautiful daughter, Princess Mah-tab-al-Bahri (Moon of the Sea). So he gave her to Rajah Suran in marriage. And three years Rajah Suran lived there. And three sons she bore him. When he saw his sons, Rajah Suran thought, "What will become of them here, under the sea? I must bring them back to my land."

So he said to Agtab-al-Ard, "If my sons grow up, will Your Majesty allow me to see that they are brought up into the upper world? This is important in order that the royal line of Sultan Iskender Dhoul-Quameen not be broken until the end of time."

"Yes," answered King Agtab-al-Ar. "I will not stop you from doing that."

Then King Agtab-al-Ar brought his horse, Sembrani, which was called Paras-al-Bahri (Sea-Horse) and gave it to Rajah Suran. And this horse carried him right up out of the sea and flew with him over the waves. When the troops of Rajah Suran saw him coming over the sea on the back of this marvelous horse, Sembrani, they led a mare to the shore. And when Sembrani saw that mare, he came to the land to meet her. Then Rajah Suran descended and Sembrani went back into the sea.

"Raise a monument here," ordered Rajah Suran, "for I wish the memory of this journey into the sea to be preserved. And write out this story, so that it may be told to all my descendants."

So a stone was set up and inscribed in the language of India. And Rajah Suran put gold, silver, and jewels under the stone.

"At the end of the centuries," he said, "there will come a king among my descendants who will find these riches. And this king will subdue every country over which the wind blows."

BADANG, THE STRONGMAN OF SINGAPURA

A Singapore Hero

Retold by Singapore storyteller Kiran Shah

*A*bout 700 years ago, there lived a young and poor slave named Badang. He worked hard from sunrise to sunset, but never had enough to eat. So every morning he would lay a fish trap in the river and every evening would hope to find a fish or two and have a bit more food to go with the little rice he was given.

One evening when he got to the river, he discovered his traps badly damaged and fish bones scattered around. He mended his traps again, only to find them ripped apart the next day. Badang was so angry he decided to find out who had been stealing his fish.

He hid among the tall bushes and waited and watched. He was almost nodding off when he heard a loud splashing from the river. There appeared a *jinn.* He had only heard about them, but now he saw one. It walked on two legs, and it looked human, with long hair and a beard, but it had the body of a fish!

But Badang was furious! *Jinn* or not, he went right up and grabbed its beard and yanked it. The *jinn* cried out to be released, but Badang would not let go. Even though the *jinn* was bigger, Badang could see that it was losing its strength away from the water.

The *jinn* pleaded to be released and promised to grant him anything. Badang thought carefully. What should he ask for? Badang thought, "If I ask for riches, my master will take it all. If I ask for the power to be invisible, they will put me to death as a sorcerer. I will ask for strength. Then I can easily do the work of my master."

"Give me strength!" decided Badung. "Let me be strong enough to tear down trees with one hand."

The *jinn* agreed to give him the strength of 10,000 elephants, on one condition. He told Badang that he would have to eat up the *jinn's* vomit, which he would spew onto a banana leaf. Badang was really disgusted. But for superhuman strength, he would do anything. Badang said he would do it. But he held tight to the *jinn's* long beard, so it could not get away. Out from deep inside the *jinn's* belly came slimy smelly remains of fish as well as *batu geliga*, stones that had magical powers. Although sickened by the sight and the smell, Badang ate it all up and immediately experienced a heat coursing through his body.

"Am I really strong?" Badang reached out with one hand and pulled up a nearby tree. "Yes! I have the strength! *Jinn,* you may go."

He released the *jinn's* beard, and the *jinn* vanished into the waters.

On the way home he pulled up every tree he saw. The huge trees he pulled up with one hand easily. And the smaller trees he just pulled up by the handfuls and tossed aside. When he reached his master's home, behind him lay an entire wilderness cleared of trees.

"Who has cleared this land?" gasped his master. "The trees and brush that covered this place have all been cleared suddenly!"

"It was I," Badang replied. And he told about his adventure with the *jinn.* His master was so impressed that he gave Badang his freedom.

Soon word of Badang's amazing strength reached the ears of Sri Rana Wikerma, who was the Rajah of Singapura at that time. Sri Rana Wikerma invited Badang to prove his strength. And Badang did so. The Rajah had ordered the construction of a ship that was so large that all the king's guards were unable to push it to the river. Badang was able to launch the boat with just a single push of his hand. Badang was made a war chief and was so helpful that he became popular throughout the land. He was given the title of Raden, or Royal Prince.

Of course word of Badang's prowess soon spread to other lands as well.

The King of Perlak had a strongman named Bandarang. "My Lord, is Badang stronger than I?" asked Bandarang. "Let me go to Singapore and challenge him!"

So the King of Perlak sent Bandarang to Singapore with the offer of a storehouse full of treasure if Badang could beat him. And a wager to receive the same from the King of Singapore, if Badang should fail.

Badang was a bit worried about this. "Your Majesty, this man is a renowned athlete. It would be a disgrace to you if he were to defeat me. If Your Majesty thinks it wise, let us both be called into your presence so that I can test him. Then if I think I can beat him, we will have the competition."

So the two strongmen were seated beside each other and served refreshments. Seated together, the two men tried each other's strength without attracting the attention of the others, who were busy drinking. Each pushed with his legs against the other. No one saw this, but the two were struggling mightily to see who could make the other yield. At the end of an hour, the King asked Badang if he was strong enough to defeat Bandarang. "Definitely," answered Badang. "We can have the competition tomorrow."

But by the next day Bandarang had changed his mind about the competition. He advised his master that Badang might win. So the minister of Perlak went to the King of Singapore with a proposition. "It is my opinion that we should prevent this struggle. If one of the contestants should be defeated in a bad way, a quarrel might arise out of it between you two kings. Let us just drop the matter." So conflict was avoided in this way.

The King of Kalinga in India also heard of Badang. He too had a strongman whom he believed was even stronger than Badang. He sent his strongman with seven ships full of treasures and issued a challenge to Badang. If Badang lost, the Rajah must give seven ships of treasures to the King of Kalinga's strongman. If Badang won, the seven ships would remain in Singapura. The challenge was accepted and the next day the competition began. There were to be three tasks. First, the two men were tested on strength by pulling an elephant. Both were found to be equally matched. Then they were tested on their speed of chopping down trees. Again, neither man was better than the other.

Their last contest took place on top of Bukit Larangan (now called Fort Canning), the abode of the Rajah. There was a giant rock, and it was agreed that whoever managed to lift it highest would be declared the winner. The strongman from Kalinga could only lift the rock up to his knees. Then it was Badang's turn. The rock was heavier than anything Badang had ever tried to lift! Slowly it started to move above his knees. Everyone in the crowd gasped in surprise. All present watched in amazement as Badang lifted the huge rock over his head. He then hurled the rock out of the palace grounds, all the way to the mouth of the Singapura River. The defeated Kalinga strongman returned home empty-handed. As for Badang, he lived on for many more years in great comfort.

Do you think it's all true? Well, Badang did exist, and so did the rock. In fact it was so big that British engineers blew it up because it was blocking the way for boats into the river. A small bit of the stone is in the Singapore History Museum, and a larger portion is in another museum in Calcutta (Kolkata), India. The bit that is in Singapore has an inscription, but no one knows what it says. I think it's all about Badang's immense powers.

HOW MALACCA GOT ITS NAME

Another episode from the Sedjaret Malayou.

*I*t is said that Iskander Shah fled Singapore after the Batara of Madjapahit overran that city. He traveled, looking for a place to stay. Iskander Shah stopped first at Moara. But there a hoard of iguanas appeared. They killed the iguanas. But the next night many more appeared. Soon the place was stinking from the rotting iguanas. The Singaporeans named the place Biaoak Bousok (putrid iguanas). And they moved on.

They came to another spot and built a fort. But during the night all that they had built was torn down. They called the place Kota-Bourok (Ruined Fort) and moved on.

At last they came to a river called Bartain. Iskander Shah stopped there at the foot of a bushy tree. He began to hunt. His hunting dog cornered a little white gazelle. But she kicked that dog right off into the water. Iskander Shah laughed. "We will build our city right here! Even the little gazelles are brave in this spot!"

"What is the name of this tree I have been leaning against?" asked Iskander Shah. He was told, "It is called a malaka tree." "Then this city shall be named 'Malaka'," proclaimed Iskander Shah. So he remained at Malaka (Malacca). And his son was Radja Besar Mouda.

THE SWORDFISH ATTACK

This episode from the Sedjaret Malayou *appears in many children's books in Singapore today.*

*I*n the time of Sultan Padouka Sri Maharadja there was a strange happening in Singapore. Suddenly one day hundreds of swordfish began to leap from the sea and attack the people. With their long sword snouts the fish would pierce clear through a man's chest. Their long noses would stab right through a man from front to back and stick out his back. People were falling injured and dying. And the attacking swordfish just kept coming.

People were running about and shouting, "The swordfish are attacking! The swordfish are attacking! They will kill us all!"

Padouka Sri Maharadja mounted his elephant and hurried to the seashore with his guards. What a sight of horror he found: dead and dying men lying all about, pierced by the swordfish. The bounding swordfish were even so wild that one of them flew high enough to pierce the sleeve of the Sultan's cloak while he was high atop his elephant.

The Sultan ordered his soldiers to stand side by side to form a rampart to keep the swordfish back. But it was useless. The swordfish just lunged at the legs of the soldiers, and they too fell. The swordfish kept coming out of the sea in unending numbers.

But one young boy spoke up. "Why make a wall of our legs? This will only get us hurt. Better to make a wall of banana tree trunks."

What a brilliant idea! A wall was made of the trunks of banana trees. These trunks are hard enough to be built into a palisade, and yet soft enough for a sword to pierce. The next time the swordfish attacked, their long, swordlike snouts struck the banana trunks, pierced them, and were stuck there! Hundreds and hundreds of swordfish flew up and impaled themselves in this way. When the swordfish had stopped leaping from the sea, the men ran out and clubbed the trapped swordfish. There were fish enough there to feed the entire populace of Singapore and still more left.

A song was composed about this event:

The boundings of the swordfish tore
The mantle which the Sultan wore.
But here they ceased their onset wild,
Thanks to the wisdom of a child.

Legends of the Sultanate of Perak

Each of the Malaysian Sultanates traces its lineage far into antiquity. Many wondrous tales have accrued to these lineages. Here are some of the legends told about the Sultanate of Perak. According to tradition, the present Sultan of Perak can trace his lineage all the way back to Alexander the Great. Perak State is located toward the northwest of the Malay peninsula, just south of Kedah State.

THE SILVER ARROW

A folktale from Perak

*S*ome say that Demang Lebar Daun, a Minangkabau chief (in Sumatera), had a magical bull. One day this bull vomited out a child! And in the child's hand was a manuscript with the coronation speech for the Sultan of Perak.

Demang Lebar Daun took his grandson and the mythical child to the top of Si Guntang Mountain. He gave his grandson a silver arrow and told him, "Shoot this arrow. Where the arrow falls, you shall be the king. You shall call that country, Perak, for the silver arrow." *Perak* means "silver."

The grandson shot the arrow and it flew straight and far. For seven days and seven nights that silver arrow flew, far across the sea, and it landed in the place where the present-day state of Perak lies.

THE LEGEND OF THE WHITE-BLOODED SEMANG GIRL

A folktale from Perak

*N*akhoda Kassim was sent by the ruler of Johore (at the tip of the Malayan peninsula) to find a site for a new settlement. He traveled north until he reached the Perak River, and there he met a group of aboriginal people, the Semang.

While Nakhoda Kassim was visiting with the Semang, one of the Semang girls cut her hand. Nakhoda Kasim saw white blood run from the cut on the girl's hand. Nakhoda Kassim was amazed at what he saw. He realized that the Semang girl must be of royal blood. In those days it was believed that royalty had white blood, unlike other people. Nakhoda Kassim was so impressed that he married the Semang girl.

Later Nakhoda Kassim sent to Johore for a prince to come rule Perak, and Sultan Muzaffar Shah came.

THE SWORD OF
ALEXANDER THE GREAT

A folktale from Perak

*T*he Sultan Mahmud of Melaka (Malacca) was driven out by the Portuguese in 1511 and fled to Johore. One of his sons became ruler of Johore. But a second son went to Perak and became the Sultan Muzaffar Shah (1528–1549), thus beginning the Perak Sultanate.

He brought with him the royal insignia, which is still used today at the installation of each new Sultan. These are royal drums, pipes, flutes, a betel box, a scepter, the seal of state, a royal umbrella, and a special sword. This sword is said to have belonged to Alexander the Great and to have been used to slay the dragon Saktimuna. The sword was also said to have been used at the installation of Parameswara, founder of the Melaka Kingdom (ca. AD 1400).

THE MAGICAL ARRIVAL OF THE DESCENDANTS OF ALEXANDER THE GREAT

A folktale from Perak

*O*ne night two widows in Sumatera saw a glow on the top of the mountain, Bukit Seguntang Mahameru, near Palembang. They thought this might be the gleam from the gem in a magical serpent's head. Next morning their rice fields had grains of pure gold!

Three young princes then appeared. The youngest was Sri Tri Buana. He was riding a white elephant and wearing royal robes and a crown. The princes said they were descendants of Alexander the Great. And to prove their lineage they pointed out the rice turned to gold, with leaves of silver and stems of gold.

It was this same Sri Tri Buana who became the first ruler of Temasek (Singapore). His descendant, Parameswara, founded Melaka. Thus the Perak Sultanate traces its heritage all the way back to Alexander the Great.

Tales of Singapore

Located at the southernmost tip of the Malay peninsula, the island of Singapore lies only miles from the Indonesian border. Our first story here shows the close ties between the islands in this region. The second story is a contemporary tale explaining the unusual cats so common in today's Singapore. And the last is a local legend about two small islands near Singapore.

THE MOST SKILLED
CARPENTER OF SINGAPORE

A folktale from Singapore

Malay peoples lived on the Malay peninsula but also lived across the straits on the island of Sumatera, and on the island of Java. Today Sumatera and Java are part of the country of Indonesia. In these old stories the kings from Java and Sumatera were often coming to the Malay peninsula, sometimes to found cities, sometimes to attack.

The King of Majapahit heard that there was a great city called Singapura, which had not submitted to him. So he sent an envoy from Java to Singapura. The envoy brought a gift. This gift was a long wood shaving, seven fathoms long, all in one piece, curled up delicately onto itself like one long piece of thin paper. It was curled like a type of earring that young women wore.

The envoy presented this marvelous wood shaving creation to the Paduka Sri Pikrama Wira, the ruler of Singapura. And he presented also a letter from the King of Majapahit, which said, "You can see here the marvelous craftsmanship of our Javanese woodworkers. Do you have any such craftsmanship in Singapura?"

Paduka Sri Pikrama Wira thought he understood the meaning of this gift. He said, "The King of Majapahit sends this wood shaving shaped like a girl's earring to mock us."

"Do not misunderstand," replied the envoy. "The King just wants to see if anyone in Singapura is as skillful as our craftsmen."

Paduka Sri Pikrama Wira then called on of his own carpenters. "We will show the King of Majapahit what a truly skilled craftsman can do with an axe!" And he ordered the man to shave a baby's head with the axe. The skilled carpenter did exactly as he was told. And so great was his skill that not a knick was made on the baby's skin, yet the baby's head was shaved smooth.

"You must agree that shaving a baby's head with an axe is even more difficult than making a wood shaving," said the King. And he sent the axe that had shaved the baby's head back to Java with the envoy.

The King of Majapahit was furious when he received this "gift." "The King of Singapura means to insult me and threaten us. By sending this axe, he says to me that if our troops attack Singapura, he will shave our heads just like the carpenter shaved the head of that baby."

The angry King of Majapahit sent troops to attack Singapura. A huge battle ensued. And in the end the Javanese had to retreat to Majapahit. The King of Singapura had in fact "shaved their heads."

THE CAT'S TAIL

A folktale from Singapore; retold by Singapore storyteller Rosemarie Somaiah

A special breed of cat lives in Singapore. The cat has a stumpy tail. Many of these cats live in the drainage ditches of Singapore and fend for themselves. They are distinctive in their appearance and easily spotted by visitors to the city. The following story is told about the origin of the Singapore cat's tail.

*T*his is the story of a princess who liked cats. She was a beautiful princess, and according to old man Kamut in the village—who is said to have told this story many, many years before I was born—she was the daughter of the great, great, great, great grandfather of the Sultan of his time.

One day, as the Sultan sat on his throne, with his courtiers around him, the Chief Minister came up to him. He bowed low and made his apologies.

"*Ampun Tuanku, beribu-ribu ampun.*" ("Apologies, Your Highness, a thousand apologies!")

"Your Highness, the princess Puteri Mawar has a request to make of you."

The Sultan nodded. "The princess is my most precious jewel, my favorite flower. Let her come to me."

The princess came in carrying Kucinta, her cat. She settled herself at the foot of her father's throne with the cat nestled in her lap. As I said, she was a beautiful princess. Dressed in the finest clothes, the princess's silky black hair shone and her smooth skin glowed. Pearls, rubies, sapphires and more gleamed from the ornaments that adorned her hair, neck, and arms. The diamonds and other precious gems in the rings on her fingers sparkled as she stroked Kucinta. But the princess was prettier by far than any precious stone. Her eyes shone brighter than any diamond, and her teeth were whiter than any pearl.

It was said that any one of the rings on her fingers alone could buy a whole kingdom, but the ministers averted their eyes.

The princess was upset. She was hot and bothered. She greeted her father, "*Ayahanda,* (formal salutation) Father, why am I not allowed to swim in the river any more?"

"*Anakanda*—my beloved daughter, you know how dangerous the river can be . . . ," began the Sultan.

"I am a good swimmer," replied the princess. "You yourself have told me I can swim better than a boy!"

"*Sang Buwaya*, the crocodile, lurks in the river," said her father.

"I am not afraid of a silly old crocodile!" said the princess, looking around the court.

"You have heard the tales of robbers and pirates that roam the islands," said her worried father. "But the river flows just beside the palace," responded the princess, "what harm can come to me? *Ayahanda*, it is such a hot day! I fear this heat will scorch my skin and wither my beauty, and you know how I love to swim in the river!"

Well, princesses will have their way, and so did she.

Soon she was making her way to the river. As the princess disrobed, her attendants spread her clothes gently down on silken cloths on a flat rock. They knew no one from the kingdom would dare come near.

Kucinta circled the princess curiously, her long tail held high. "Miaow," she said. "Kucinta, you want to swim in the river?" "Miaow," replied Kucinta, drawing away.

Suddenly, as the princess began to take off her precious jewelry, she had an idea.

"Come here, Kucinta!" She slipped all of her beautiful rings onto the cat's tail. "You are my closest companion, Kucinta. You are as beautiful as a princess yourself. Keep my jewelry safe!" Then, just to be sure, she knotted the end of the tail and slipped into the cool waters of the river, followed by her attendants. Kucinta wandered around and settled down for a nap.

Now, it happened that some pirates from a neighboring island had been lurking in the area. Hiding in the bushes, they watched carefully till the princess and her attendants were swimming in the middle of the river some distance from the banks. Then they sneaked out to steal the jewels.

But Kucinta the cat had heard the rustling in the bushes. With her stomach and tail held low, she crept away stealthily into the long grass.

Before the princess and her attendants out in the river had seen what had happened or could do anything about it, the pirates escaped with most of the jewels. Everything was gone—everything, except the rings still safe on Kucinta's tail!

Well, the Sultan was certainly relieved that his precious daughter was safe. But the princess did feel sorry.

"Kucinta kept my rings safe, but look, *Tuan Ku*! Her tail is bent and will not be straight again!"

"Well," said the Sultan, "Kucinta has served you well. Remember never to hurt a cat again. From now on, cats in this region will have a knot in their tails. Let it be known forever that this is a mark of distinction—an honor—for loyalty and service to the kingdom."

And so it has been from that day on till today . . . to those who have heard this story.

If you look at the cats that roam around Singapore today, you will find that most of them still carry that mark of honor—the knot in the tail!

SISTERS ISLAND

A folktale from Singapore; retold by Singapore storytellers Kiran Shah, Panna Kantilal, and Jessie Goh

*I*magine a long time ago when you were not born, your parents were not born, your grandparents were not born, and even your great grandparents were not born. In fact Singapore wasn't even called Singapore. It was called Temasek. It was mainly a fishing village just like the other islands around it.

On one of these outer islands there was a small village. In this village a poor widow lived with her two daughters, Minah and Linah. Their father had died when they very young. It was a hard life, and the mother struggled to feed them all. As they grew older, they helped her in her vegetable garden, growing tapioca, sweet potatoes, and chilies. They would go into the jungle to pick fruit. Coconuts and bananas were plentiful, but they always looked forward to picking the *rambutans, durians,* and *mangosteens* when these were in season. They also learned to fish from the rocks. Everything they did, they did together. They led a simple but happy life, playing games like "five stones" and *"ting ting"* (hop scotch). They were inseparable.

Their mother would constantly worry about them, especially about their future when she would no longer be around. Minah, the elder of the two sisters, would always comfort her, telling her that she would look after her younger sister Linah.

As they reached their teens, their mother told them that it was time for them to get married, so that their husbands could look after them. Then she could die in peace. But the two sisters didn't want to be separated. So they told their mother they would only get married to two brothers and that way they need not be separated. Their mother reluctantly agreed, and word went out to all the other outlying islands and even to the big island of Temasek. Many suitors came, as they had heard not only of the sisters' beauty but also of their kind, gentle ways.

But none of them were brothers, and the sisters rejected every one.

Not long after, their mother died, leaving the sisters no choice but to live with their uncle on another island. The two sisters grew even closer together, renewing their vow to remain together always.

Things were never the same. The villagers on this island lived in constant fear of the *orang laut*, the people of the sea, some of whom were pirates. One day, as Linah was drawing water from the well, a shadow fell over her and she looked up to see a big, burly, fierce-faced man looking at her. She ran in terror, only to hear his booming voice say, "Follow her, I have found my bride!"

Linah rushed home and collapsed into Minah's arms. "*Tolong Kak*" ("Help, sister!") , "*Tolong, Pakchik*" ("Help, Uncle!"), was all she could keep repeating. Then a voice was heard outside their door. Their uncle went out and some conversation ensued. He came back, looked at the two sisters, and said helplessly, "That was the chief of the pirates. He intends to come tomorrow to take Linah away as his bride." Linah and Minah cried out," Do something, *Pakchik*." But their uncle could not help. He was powerless against the pirate chief, and the villagers would suffer if the pirate's wish was not granted. The sisters did not sleep that night. They just clung to one another, not knowing what to do.

The next morning, as the sun rose, the pirate chief and his men were back in the village. They dragged Linah toward the shore, where their *sampan* was moored.

All the villagers watched helplessly as Minah ran after the chief and pleaded, "Let my sister go! I beg of you. *Lepaskan dia*!" Her cries were ignored, and she watched helplessly as Linah was lifted into the boat. She heard Linah crying out to her, "*Tolong!* You promised that we would not be separated! *Tolong!*"

And then to her horror Minah saw her sister wriggle free and fling herself into the raging waters. Without a thought, Minah plunged in, too. They were never seen again.

The next day, the villagers saw something they had not seen before. Two strange-looking humps that formed two islands were seen at the very place where Linah and Minah had disappeared beneath the waves. These two islands were named Sisters Island in memory of the two sisters who were inseparable till the very end.

MAT JENIN AND THE COCONUTS

A Malay tale from Singapore

A man named Semordan owned a great number of coconut trees. When he saw that many of the coconuts were ripe, he sent for a man by the name of Mat Jenin. Mat Jenin was well known in the area of Singapura as a skilled climber of coconut trees

But Mat Jenin was a shrewd bargainer. "Hmmm. If I climb these trees and pick your coconuts, how much will you pay me?"

Semordan looked at the crop of ripe coconuts. "Well, Mat Jenin, if you climb the trees and pick my coconuts, I will give you two coconuts from each tree you climb." This seemed like a good deal to Mat Jenin. He started at once to climb the first tree.

"Two coconuts from each tree," thought Mat Jenin. He looked around and began to count the trees. "One, two, . . ." There were twenty-five trees! "Twenty-five times two, that means I will get fifty coconuts!"

Mat Jenin began to plan. "I will sell the coconuts, and with the money I will buy chickens. My hens will lay eggs. The eggs will hatch. I will have many chickens!"

Mat had climbed quickly and reached the top of the first tree. But his mind was racing. "I will sell the chickens and buy DUCKS! The ducks will lay eggs. I will have more ducks!"

Mat Jenin absentmindedly began to pick the coconuts and let them drop to the ground far below. In the top of the tall coconut tree he was lost in his daydream.

"I will sell the ducks and buy GOATS! The goats will have kids. I will have a large flock of goats! I will drive them down the road to sell them. I will have to wave my arms and shout. "Move, goats! Move on!" And forgetting where he was, Mat Jenin began to wave his arms and shout at his imaginary goats.

Alas, that was the end of his daydream. For Mat Jenin lost his grip on the coconut tree and fell crashing to the ground himself.

And that was the end of Mat Jenin and his daydream.

Malay Place Legends

    Traveling around Malaysia, one finds amazing stories attached to every island, mountain, lake, and promontory. In this section are tales from the island of Langkawi, from Lake Chini in the Malaysian state of Pahang, Mount Ophir (Gunong Ledang), which stands between Malacca and Johore, the city of Palembang, and Batu Gadjah, a rock formation in Perak State.

THE LEGEND OF THE BEAUTIFUL MAHSURI AND HER SEVEN-GENERATION CURSE

A folktale from Langkawi

Langkawi and its surrounding islands are located near the Thai and Malaysian border. This was a quiet, rural island until recently, when tourism began to bring development to the island.

*O*nce, long ago, a beautiful girl was born to two Thai immigrants who were living on Langkawi. The child was called Mahsuri, and she grew to be both kind and lovely. In time she was married to Wan Darus, son of the Chief of Langkawi. But Wan Darus was sent off to fight an invading army from Thailand. And while he was gone, a traveling minstrel and poet named Deraman came to Langkawi. Mahsuri loved his storytelling, and he and she became good friends. It is said that she even allowed him to stay at her home while he was in town. This was a mistake. Gossip began that Mahsuri was unfaithful to her husband. Her mother-in-law had been jealous of Mahsuri, and this gave her an excuse to persuade her husband, Dato Karma Jayo, to execute the girl.

Mahsuri was tied to a tree and attacked with swords and knives, but nothing could harm her. She seemed magically protected. This should have shown the people that she was indeed innocent. But they would not relent. At last she resigned herself to her fate and told them that she could be killed only by a special kris (a ceremonial dagger) kept at her own home. The kris was brought, . . . the sky grew black, . . . thunder and lightning reigned, . . . and Mahsuri was killed. From her body flowed white blood. Seeing this, the people realized that she had been innocent. But it was too late now. And in her dying breath Mahsuri had cursed the island, saying that Langkawi would not prosper for seven generations to come, their punishment for this injustice.

Not long after her death, Thailand invaded Langkawi. In an attempt to starve the invaders, Dato Karma Jaya ordered all of the rice on the island collected and burned at Padang Mat Sirat. This turned out to be a foolish act, since now the islanders themselves had nothing to eat and began to die of starvation. They say that grains of burnt rice still appear after rainy days, magically emerging from the ground at Padang Mat Sirat, where the evil burning of the rice took place. And for many generations after Langkawi was sparsely settled. It became a remote backwater with few inhabitants.

As for the curse of Mahsuri, in the year 2000 the government managed to locate the descendants of Mahsuri, who had returned to Thailand. They were living on the island of Phuket. They were brought to Langkawi and invited to make Langkawi their home. They chose to return to Phuket. But it is said that with the birth of an eighth-generation descendant of Mahsuri in 1980, the fortunes of the island of Langkawi at last began to change.

Note: *A painting of Mahsuri and a photo of her eighth-generation ancestor may be seen online at http://www.abcmalaysia.com/tour_malaysia/lgkwi_mahsuri.htm.*

THE ORIGIN OF LAKE CHINI

A folktale from Pahang

*I*n the province of Pahang lies a large lake known as Lake Chini. Many legends are told about this lake.

It is said that long ago an aborigine group came to the area where the lake is now and began to clear land. They were using digging sticks to make holes in the ground to plant crops. Out of the forest came an old woman leaning on a walking stick. "What are you people doing here on my land?" They explained that they did not know the area was inhabited. They had come to plant some crops here. "Well, you should have asked my permission. This is my land, you know. You can't just come out and start clearing someone else's land."

The people apologized and humbly asked the old woman's permission to plant there. "Very well. Since you ask properly, you may plant here." But before the old woman left she planted her walking stick in the middle of the field. "Do not pull this stick from my ground," she warned them. "Not now. Not EVER." And she disappeared.

Some time later a dog began to bark at a rotting log on the edge of the clearing. One of the men threw his dibble stick at the log. Blood spurted out. When his friends came and saw the barking dog and the bleeding log they laughed and threw more dibble sticks at the log. Soon blood was gushing out and flowing away across the ground. But the men just laughed at the bleeding log.

Suddenly the sky was split with lightning, and thunder began to roll. The skies let loose a downpour of rain and everyone ran for cover. In the turmoil the old woman's walking stick was knocked out of the ground. Now water began to gush from the hole where the stick had stood. The earth began to shake and became very soft. People were overtaken by the water. They ran here and there, but everywhere they ran, the water followed. A huge lake was formed, Tasek Chini. And everywhere the people ran, today rivulets lead off from the lake.

They say that one old man escaped from the disaster. And it was he who told this story.

THE NAGA DRAGONS OF LAKE CHINI

A folktale from Pahang

*I*n later years other tales were told of the magical Lake Chini. There were said to be two Naga (akin to dragons) who lived in Tasek Chini. On dark nights, when the Pahang River was in flood, they would come out of the lake and go downstream. Villagers would hear thunder and lightning as they passed.

One day, as the naga were swimming out into the South China Sea, the female naga realized that she had forgotten her sash. So she swam back to Tasek Chini to get it. Her husband swam on into the sea without her. She went back to the lake and fetched her sash, but by the time she came back to the sea, her husband was far ahead of her.

Unfortunately the lady naga swam too close to an island, Bukit Dato. Her sash got caught on a stone. She tried and tried to free herself. She called to her husband to come help, but he was too far away to hear. Then, while she was trying to get free, she heard the cock crow. They say a cock rode on her back! At any rate, when she heard the cock crow, she knew it was almost daylight and she could not go farther. So she stayed right where she was and became an island, Pulau Tioman.

Her husband naga had swam on ahead. But he also heard the cock crow. So he stopped too. And he became Pulau Daik.

You can visit those two islands if you like, Pulau Tioman and Pulau Daik.

THE GREAT WHITE
CROCODILE

A folktale from Pahang

*I*n Tasek Chini there lived also a great white crocodile. His name was Seri Pahang (The Glory of Pahang). Seri Pahang heard about a devastating black monster, Seri Kemboja (The Glory of Kemboja). He vowed to fight the monster and get rid of him. So Seri Pahang left Tasek Chini and swam downstream to Kuala Pahang. There he changed himself into an old man carrying a dipper. In the form of the old man, Seri Pahang persuaded a crew of boatmen to take him on board with them. Since he had a dipper, they thought he might be useful if the boat needed to be bailed. His dipper seemed to have turmeric (a golden-colored spice) in it.

When the boat reached a spot southeast of Sedili Kechil, Seri Pahang handed the dipper to one of the men and jumped into the sea! Immediately he turned back into a giant white crocodile. And the men were amazed to see that the turmeric in the dipper had turned to gold! This was their payment for giving Seri Pahang a ride to the spot where he wanted to challenge Seri Kemboja, the black monster.

The fight between Seri Pahang, the great white crocodile, and Seri Kemboja, the black monster, lasted long. The sea became dark. Thunder rolled and lightning flashed. After much fighting, Seri Pahang managed to drive Seri Kemboja away. But in the fight, Seri Pahang was mortally wounded. He swam away to Pulau Aur (Aur Island) and clung to the rudder of a boat that was going back to Kuala Pahang. Once he reached Sekukoh on the Pahang River, Seri Pahang let go of the rudder. He told the people there to take a message to his people up at Lake Chini. If they wanted to see him before he died, they should come right away to Sekukoh.

The boat with the message traveled to Kuala Chini. But the boatmen forgot to deliver the message. When they tried to pole farther upriver, though, the boat would not move. At last they remembered the message. As soon as it was delivered, the boat could move again.

Soon hundreds of crocodiles could be seen swimming downriver to Sekukoh. People say there were so many crocodiles in the river that a man could cross the river stepping on their backs. Before he died, Seri Pahang, the great white crocodile, asked the ruler of Pahang to give him a proper Muslim burial. And so this was done.

In 1914, when Sultan Ahmad died, people saw twenty-six crocodiles cruising in a "V" formation, heading upriver. Behind them came a shoal of fish fanned out across the river. The people cast nets, but the fish magically escaped. They were a type of fish that usually lives in Lake Chini. The people believed that the crocodiles and fish were coming back from the funeral of Almarhum Sultan Ahmad. They had been paying their respects in gratitude, because the Sultan's ancestor had buried Seri Pahang properly at Sekukoh when he died.

THE PRINCESS OF GUNONG LEDANG (MOUNT OPHIR)

A folktale from Johore

*T*he Sultan Mansur Shah ruled the Sultanate of Malacca well. But once he got a strange idea into his head. He had heard that a beautiful princess lived on the top of Gunong Ledang. This mountain was then in the Sultanate of Malacca. Now it is in the State of Johore. It is now called Mount Ophir.

Back in those long ago days, the mountain was very hard to reach. The Sultan sent high officials to go to the mountain top to bring his request that the princess become his wife. The officials brought with them men from Indragiri who could help them find the way up the mountain. But even with this help, the officials soon gave up. So Tun Mamad offered to go on with two friends.

It is said that a strong wind was blowing on the mountaintop. They passed a grove of singing bamboo trees, and the wind in the bamboos made such beautiful music that even birds came down to listen. Tun Mamad and his friends rested in this grove of singing bamboo. And then they continued their climb.

When they reached the home of the princess, four old women met them in the garden. Tun Mamad stepped forward and told them his mission. "I come from the Sultan Mansur Shah. He would like to marry the Princess of Gunong Ledang."

"I am Dang Raya Rani," replied the woman in charge. "I am the guardian of the Princess of Gunong Ledang. I will take your message to her."

The four old women disappeared into the house. And Tun Mamad and his men waited. After a while a very old woman appeared. She was much older than the other women. And she was bent over with age. Some say that she was really the Princess of Gunong Ledang in disguise. But she appeared to be merely a very old woman to the men.

"Your message has been given to the Princes of Gunong Ledang," she stated. "And this is her reply, 'If the Sultan of Malacca wants to marry me, he must do the following:

Build a bridge of gold and silver stretching from Malacca to Gunong Ledang.

Send as wedding gifts:

> seven trays of mosquito hearts
>
> seven trays of mites' hearts
>
> a vat of young areca-nut water
>
> a vat of tears
>
> and a cup of his son's blood.

If he does all this, I will marry him'."

Tun Mamad and his men hurried back down the mountain and took this message to the Sultan. When he heard these requests he was stunned. Finally he shook his head in resignation and spoke.

"I could perhaps do all of these things, difficult though they are," he said. "But I could never take a cup of my young son's blood."

The Sultan turned to his messengers. "Send word to the princess. I am afraid I cannot marry her after all."

And so the Sultan wisely gave up on his foolish quest to woo the Princess of Gunong Ledang.

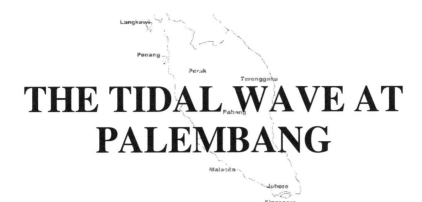

THE TIDAL WAVE AT PALEMBANG

A folktale from Sumatera

*I*n early times Sumatera was ruled by three magical kings. They were Encik Darat, King of the Earth; Encik Alun, Lord of the Waves; and Sang Burung, Master of the Seasons.

Together they worked to create a peaceful and prosperous country. But there came a time when some humans were taking more than others. Rich people were taking all of the wealth for themselves, while the poor became worse and worse off.

Encik Darat saw this and called the two other kings together. He wanted to punish the rich for the power they were grabbing. But Sang Burung would not believe that the humans were behaving in that way. He refused to agree. Encik Darat was exasperated. He turned Sang Burung into an owl! "Go roam the world at night then, and see what you see!"

Once Sang Burung was gone, the other two kings didn't have much to say. Sang Burung was the one who always had the clever ideas for them.

Meanwhile Sang Burung flew to the city of Palembang to see if the things Encik Darat had said were true. There he saw the poor people living on the outskirts of town in very sad conditions. At the city center the rich were feasting and drinking lavishly. "I will test their hearts," thought Sang Burung. So he turned himself into an old beggar and entered the village. The feasting rich tried to drive him away. But he spoke up. "I can show you something. I will bet you gold that you cannot pull this from the ground." And bending over, he planted a stalk of grass in the earth.

The rich men threw down their drinks and came to pull out the grass stalk and win the gold. But no matter who tried, no matter how hard they pulled, the blade of grass would not come out.

At last Sang Burung bent down and pulled up the blade of grass. "You rich people of Palembang have no strength, because you have no strength of character. You live in luxury and never give one penny to the poor. You can no more pull a grass stalk from the earth than

---

you can open your hearts to give a bowl of rice to others. We will wash your wealth away with water. All that you have now is wasted."

And Sang Burung turned back into an owl and flew away. In the heavens he met with the other two kings. "You were right, Encik Darat. The rich of Palembang are heartless. Encik Alun, it is time to wash these wicked rich men away."

So Encik Alun called upon the sea, which he ruled. And the sea rose up in a mighty wave and attacked Palembang. And the mansions of the rich were all washed out to sea.

To this day the wicked fear the owl. And to this day men look to the sea and worry. Will Encik Alun become angry again?

Note: In 2004 a tidal wave struck the island of Sumatera and caused enormous destruction in Banda Aceh. Perhaps this story was created to explain a similar event.

THE LEGEND OF BATU GADJAH

A folktale from Perak

With thanks to Mohd. Taib b. Mohamed of Ipoh, and children's librarian Suraya Arrifin, who lives at Batu Gadjah, Perak.

A great tragedy once occurred. A man was cutting trees by the side of the Kinta River when a tree fell onto his child, and the child was killed. This man began to wail in his great grief. "Why, oh why? My son, my son." Of course the man was beside himself with grief.

Some elephants were bathing in the river nearby. They were annoyed at the man's loud wailing. "Stop making such a racket, man!" They called.

"But my son has been killed," sobbed the man.

The elephants had no pity in their hearts. "Why cry about that?" said one of the elephants. "Just be glad it fell on your child and not on you." And the rest of the elephants echoed this sentiment. "Don't be a cry baby. It's only a child that got killed."

The man was enraged at the insensitivity of these elephants. "You are lucky I can keep my tongue," muttered the man. "Or else."

"Or else what?" taunted the elephants. "Just what would you say?"

"Here is what I would say to you cruel-hearted elephants. I would curse you to turn into stones."

And so deep was the man's anger, that his curse became fact. Those coldhearted elephants were stopped in their tracks, turned into stones as cold as their hearts.

The rock still stands there today; it is called "Batu Gadjah" (Elephant Rock), and the village nearby also bears that name, Batu Gadjah.

Magical Tales

Many Malay tales contain unusual magical elements. The four tales in this section are especially wondrous in the imagination of their creators. We have first an elephant princess, then a fairy princess who leaves when wronged, a magical spinning top that leads the way to adventure, and finally an unusual fighting cock.

THE ELEPHANT PRINCESS

A folktale from Pattani

*I*n the olden days the Prophet Adam quarreled with the Lady Eve and they decided to live apart. So Adam went to live by the sea coast, but the Lady Eve crossed the sea on a bridge made of soap-vine stem and became Queen there.

Now in time she gave birth to a beautiful daughter. When the Princess grew up, the Queen warned her that if she ever crossed the waters on the soap-vine bridge, she must promise never to mess up the fields of the people there. But one day the Princess did cross over the soap-vine bridge. And forgetting all about her mother's warnings, she wandered about and smashed up things in the fields of sugarcane and corn and bananas there. And oh my! She was turned into an elephant! And of course as an elephant she REALLY began to tear up the crops!

Now a Prince was studying at a temple nearby, and seeing the great beast trampling the fields, he struck her in the center of the forehead with his pike. The point of the pike broke off in the elephant's head, but she rampaged away and escaped back across the soap-vine bridge to her own country.

The Prince returned to the temple and told the Wise Man there what had happened. The Wise Man explained that this must have been a Princess in disguise. So the Prince set out to track her. On arriving at the country on the other side of the soap-vine bridge, he went right to the palace. Sure enough, the Princess was ill in bed.

The Prince asked that a special room be built where he could treat the Princess. And when he was alone with the Princess, he secretly removed the iron point from her forehead and hid it in a bamboo tube. Then he patted the Princess and blew into her face until she awoke. Of course, since he had healed the Princess, he was given her hand in marriage.

The two lived happily for some time. But eventually the Prince took the Princess across the soap-vine bridge to visit his own country. She followed him, with a train of thirty-nine handmaidens to accompany her. Unfortunately, once she had crossed the bridge, she could not resist running into the fields again. And her handmaidens all rampaged through the fields behind her. So alas, since they were trampling about like elephants, the Princess and all of her handmaidens were turned into elephants!

Note: This story was collected in Pattani, now a province of Southern Thailand. In Pattani live both Thai and Malay peoples. The prince in the story appears to have been studying at a Buddhist temple.

THE PRINCESS OF UMBRELLA HILL: PUTERI BUKIT PAYUNG

A folktale from Terengganu; retold by Kimini Ramachandran

*O*nce upon a time there lived a poor farmer named Pak Putih. He lived with his wife, Mak Siti, and their only daughter, Melati, in the small village of Bukit Payung, or Umbrella Hill. Melati was about to get married very soon, and her parents were busy making arrangements for her wedding.

One afternoon, Pak Putih left his work in the fields early to go over to his neighbor's house and borrow some plates for the wedding feast. No one had any good dishes or silverware, but they would loan each other what they had, and by borrowing from neighbors they could get together enough things to serve their feast. As Mak Siti walked back home through the jungle from their plot of farm land, she began to worry about Melati's impending wedding. They could perhaps borrow a few plates from the neighbor. But where would they get enough things to serve everyone at the wedding feast?

Suddenly Mak Siti felt as if someone was watching her from the bushes. "Who is there?" she called out. A soft and melodious voice replied, "I am over here, Mak Siti." A lovely maiden with long black hair and shining skin stood in the clearing. "I am *Puteri Bukit Payung*, the Princess of Umbrella Hill, and I know the villagers' plight. I have often marveled at how you help each other at times of need. Do not worry, Mak Siti, I will help not only you but all those in your village who need to prepare for a celebratory feast. I will ensure that you will find everything that you need right here, at this spot. All I ask in return is for those who use my things to return them in their original condition. If anything is broken, it must be replaced by the borrower." With that the Princess told Mak Siti to return to this very spot the next day and she would find all that she needed for the feast.

True enough, the next day, when Mak Siti, Pak Putih, and Melati went to the clearing in the jungle, they were astonished to find all the plates, dishes, cups, glasses, and spoons that they would need for the feast.

On the day of Melati's wedding, the villagers were surprised to see the brand new, sparkling glasses and plates laid out on the table. They knew that Pak Putih and Mak Siti were poor, just like them, and their belongings old, stained, and cracked. So Mak Siti told them about the Princess and her one request, that they return her things in good condition. The villagers quickly promised to be careful with the Princess's goods.

From that day on, whenever there was a feast or celebration of any sort, the villagers would miraculously find everything they needed in the clearing in the jungle. At first, they were very careful with what they borrowed, making sure every item was cleaned properly and treated with care and returned in its original condition. But as time passed, the villagers became careless and forgot the promise made to the Princess *Puteri Bukit Payung*. Plates were broken, dishes were chipped, glasses cracked, spoons and cups lost, and nothing was replaced.

When it came to the day when Pak Putih and Mak Siti wanted to celebrate the birth of their first grandchild, they hurried back to the clearing. But there was nothing there except shards of broken glass and pieces of cracked porcelain. They called out to the Princess. "*Puteri Bukit Payung! Puteri Bukit Payung*! Where are our party dishes?" But nobody appeared or answered.

The villagers felt bad and regretted what they had done. But it was too late, they had not kept their promise. From that day on, the people of Bukit Payung had to resort to borrowing each other's old and stained cutlery and crockery to celebrate any occasion, just like they had to do before they met the princess *Puteri Bukit Payung*.

It seems that even a fairy princess cannot help those who will not help themselves.

THE SINGING TOP

A folktale from Perak

In some parts of Malaysia young men love to play a game called gasing. This is played with a large wooden top. The men wrap a cord tightly around the top and then throw it very hard at a certain spot on the ground. If thrown well, the top will spin steadily in that spot for a very long time. Some say that good top players have thrown tops that would spin for over an hour.

*J*n Kampung Mengkudu Kuning there once lived a young man who was exceptional at playing *gasing*. When he threw his top, it would spin and spin, often much longer than the other players' tops. He took special care of his top. And when he spun it, it seemed that it actually spoke. It seemed that it sang *mengkudu kuning, mengkudu kuning, mengkudu kuning*. This was the name of the village. The village was named for the yellow mengkudu fruit, because so many of these delicious fruited trees grew around the village. So the top could also be thought to be singing "yellow mengkudu, yellow mengkudu, yellow mengkudu." It was maybe singing about the delicious yellow fruit.

Now the Rajah heard of this amazing singing top. So he sent for the young man to be brought to the palace. "Let me hear your top sing!" commanded the Raja.

The young man threw the top. "*Mengkudu kuning, mengkudu kuning*," sang the top. And then it began to talk! "Jungle, jungle, tree, tree, *puteri, puteri*."

Puteri means princess. The Rajah bent to listen more closely. And suddenly the top began to chant a *pantun*, a poem!

> *Nyior manis tepi pengkalan,*
> *Tempat merak bersarang tujoh.*
> *Hitam manis turun berjalan,*
> *Bagai kilat bintang sa-puloh.*

Sweet coconut at the jetty's edge,
Where seven peacocks nest.
My dark girl is walking,
Bright as ten shining stars.

The Rajah was entranced. "Go at once!" he ordered. "Take your talking top, and find this beautiful princess. Bring her to me. She will be a bride for my son!"

The young man was in trouble now. How could he find a princess in some far-off jungle? He left the palace and started walking through the forest. But it seemed hopeless. At last he stopped to rest. He took his top out, looked at it, and threw it. As soon as the top began to spin, it started to speak again. "Follow the path . . . a coconut grove, tallest tree, that is the place."

So he set out again. And after a long time traveling along the path, sure enough, there was a coconut grove. And in the middle of the grove was a tall, tall tree.

A sweet feminine voice sang down from the treetop:

Chinchin permata batu-nya retak,
Pakaian anak Rajah Muda,
Musim durian rambutan masak,
Manggis menumpang bertarok muda.

Ring with a cracked gem.
Worn by Rajah Muda's son.
Durian in season. Rambutan is ripe.
Mangosteen is only green.

The young man laughed. The *pantun* poem meant, "You can't have everything at once." He replied in verse:

From Pulau Indera Sakti
I come to ask one thing.
The Rajah sends me here,
to bring his son a bride.

There was laughter from the treetop. Then a ladder was lowered down the tree, and a beautiful young maiden lightly descended.

"I am glad to see you come for me. My father has said that the one I should marry would come. I am Puteri Kelapa Gading. Welcome, my husband to be."

"No! You misunderstand. I come to take you as bride for the Rajah's son."

But Puteri Kelapa Gading simply smiled and shook her head.

"My father has said, 'The one who comes to find you, that is the one you will marry'."

What a predicament. Of course he couldn't help falling in love with this beautiful creature. But what to do?

He picked up his top and spun it.

Round and round whirled the top. And it seemed to say, "honesty, trust, honesty, trust."

So he brought the beautiful Puteri Kelapa Gading back to the Rajah's court. He confessed to the Rajah all that had happened.

The Rajah was furious. This girl was to be the bride of his own son, not that of some village boy. But fortunately there was a wise man in the Raja's court. He could see that Puteri Kelapa Gading was no ordinary girl. She came from the special yellow coconut tree. Her name, "Kelapa Gading" meant "yellow coconut." And it was clear that she wanted to marry the young man from the village of the yellow mengkudu fruit. "It might be dangerous to our land to deny this woman her choice of husband," advised the elder. "I suspect she is of magical ancestry." So the Rajah acceded. "Very well, I will find another bride for my son."

The Rajah announced to all, "The princess Puteri Kelapa Gading has chosen a husband. She will marry the brave young man from the village of Mengkudu Kuning!"

And so it was.

They say that whenever the young man threw his top after that, it hummed only one thing: "*mengkudu kuning . . . mengkugu kuning . . . mengkudu kuning.*" But sometimes, if he threw the top very, very hard, it would seem to jump for joy, and would hum: "*kelapa gading . . . kelapa gading . . . kelapa gading.*"

Pulau Indera Sakti is the island on which the first Sultan of Perak set foot when he came from Malacca. Each new Sultan must dip his foot in the water there when he is installed. The Malay pantun *is a poetic form often used in courtship. The boy and girl would chant enigmatic or riddle poems back and forth to each other.*

The types of fruit named in the pantun *are tropical fruit considered delicious in this area. The* durian *is a large fruit, bigger than a cantaloupe, which exudes a really foul smell when opened. But its flavor is delicious. It has been compared to eating the world's most delicious ambrosia while sitting in a stinky toilet.* Rambutan *is a strange fruit with bright red, hairy-looking skin. Once opened, it reveals a delicious, milky white fruit, about the size of a large plum. The* mangosteen *has a similar delicious fruit inside a tough smooth, brown skin, which can be popped open if squeezed in a certain way.*

The Singing Top

AYAM JANTAM BERBULU TIGAL: THE THREE-FEATHERED ROOSTER

A folktale from Perlis; retold by Kamini Ramachandran

*O*nce upon a time in a small village in the north of Malaysia, there was a poor, orphan boy named Awang. Awang lived alone, with hardly any friends. One day, as he was foraging for food in the jungle, he came across a nest with a single chicken egg. Awang saw that the egg was about to hatch. He waited until the chick emerged from the shell. He looked around for a mother hen. He listened for the sounds of clucking of a mother hen. But after some time Awang realized the chick was all alone, just like him, and so he decided to take the chick back home with him and look after it as his pet.

In time, the little chick grew up into a rooster. He was magnificent in every way, with long, sharp claws; a fine upright, bright red comb on his head; and a strong, yellow, curved beak. Awang's rooster was magnificent in every way except one: He had no feathers at all! The rooster was all skin and no feathers! But Awang loved his pet and cared for him every day.

One day, Awang noticed that his rooster had sprouted three feathers! Yes, just three feathers. One feather at the tip of each wing, and one feather on its bottom! So he named his rooster "Ketukung Togel," which referred to his bald state. He began to train Ketukung Togel in the art of cockfighting.

After many weeks, when Ketukung Togel was well trained, Awang decided to go to the neighboring land of Siam. During his journey, everyone he passed laughed at his rooster and kept pointing at the strange-looking bird. Awang was unhappy, and he hid his pet under his *kain selempang,* his shoulder sash.

Halfway through his journey, Awang met an old man. Awang told the old man of his plans to enter Ketukung Togel in a cockfight. But the old man asked, "And what will you use as a wager for the fight?" Poor Awang had not thought about the wager, so he explained to the old man how he had nothing. "In that case, enter the competition wagering your heart and soul," said the old man. Awang thanked the old man and continued on his journey to Siam.

In time Awang reached the Southern Province of Siam. He joined the huge crowd watching the cockfights going on. In the end, there was only one rooster left standing alive, and it belonged to the Ruler of this Province. The Ruler called out, "Is there anybody else who dares challenge my rooster, Beliring Emas?" At this point, Awang stepped forward into the arena and placed Ketukung Togel on the earth. Everybody began to laugh! "What is your wager?" asked the Ruler. "I wager all that I have, Sir! And since I have nothing, I wager my heart and soul!" said Awang. The crowd was silent, amused at this unknown boy with his strange-looking rooster daring to compete with Beliring Emas. The Ruler nodded his head and agreed to Awang's wager. Then Awang asked, "Sir, what will be your wager for this competition?" The Ruler began to laugh and he was so sure his rooster would win the fight, he said, "I wager all my winnings as well as my Province!"

The cockfighting competition began, and all eyes were on the newcomer, Ketukung Togel. Poor Ketukung Togel was rolling around on the sand, and Beliring Emas was scratching the ground with its claws like a true winner, when all of a sudden Ketukung Togel leapt into the air and plunged his claws into the other rooster, killing it! The crowd was shocked and silent for a while, and then they burst into a roar of applause and lifted Awang on their shoulders, declaring him the winner! The Ruler had no choice but to hand over his entire winnings as well as the rights to the Province to Awang.

But Awang returned the money to the people of that Province and declared that from that day onwards, there would be no more cockfighting in that land. The people cheered and clapped their hands and carried Awang all the way to the Ruler's residence. Ketukung Togel now had a new home, just like his master, Awang. And as for the cockfight-loving Ruler, he disappeared from that land and was never heard of again.

Tales of Kancil the Mouse Deer

Tales of the tiny Kancil are popular in Malaysia and Indonesia. This tiny animal is not really a deer and not quite as small as a mouse. It is less than a foot and a half tall and does look a bit like a short-legged deer, though it has no horns and instead has little tusks! In stories, the tiny Kancil always tricks the bigger forest animals. Here are three Kancil trickster stories and one other, well-known story, in which Kancil gets into trouble. Because Malaysia is a country with an Islamic heritage, King Solomon, here called Suleiman, figures in these stories.

The current Malay spelling is Kancil. The Indonesian spelling is Kantjil. The name is also spelled Kantchil in some sources. The pronunciation of all is Kän-chill. Another Malay name for this tiny creature is Pelandok.

KANCIL AND SANG BUWAYA

*K*ancil Mouse Deer needed to go down to the river to drink every day. But this was difficult because Sang Buyawya, the Crocodile, lived in the river.

One day when Kancil came to the river, he saw a log floating out in the middle of the stream. It *looked* like a log . . . but it *might* be a crocodile.

Kancil was afraid to drink.

Then he had an idea.

He began to speak loudly, "I can easily find out whether that is a log or a crocodile. If that is a *log*, it will float *upstream*. If it is a *crocodile*, it will float *downstream*."

Now of course, a log could never float upstream. The river current would carry it downstream.

But Sang Buwaya did not know this.

Kancil watched.

Slowly the log began to move UPSTREAM.

"Ahhh," said Kancil. "I think I will not drink here today."

He called out, "Hey, Sang Buwaya, logs do not float UPSTREAM! Good-bye, Sang Buwaya. I FOOLED YOU!"

Another day when Kancil came down to drink, he did not see Sang Buwaya anywhere. "I think it is safe to wade into the water today," thought Kancil. He waded into the water and began to drink.

But suddenly, WHUNK! Sang Buwaya grabbed onto the leg of the little Mouse Deer! It hurt like anything! But Kancil just called out, "Sorry, Sang Buwaya, you think that is my leg, but that is just a root you are biting!"

The crocodile let loose of Kancil's leg and bit hard on something else.

Sang Buwaya was biting on a root now, but Kancil began to cry out: "Oh oh oh! You are biting my leg! Stop! Stop, Sang Buwaya!"

The crocodile just held on harder than ever. And Kancil was able to jump back out of the water and limp home on his wounded little leg.

As he left he called out, "Hey, Sang Buwaya! You are biting on a ROOT! Good-bye, Sang Buwaya! I FOOLED YOU!"

One day Kancil smelled ripe mangoes. They were hanging on a tree across the river. He really wanted to eat those mangoes. But how could he get across?

"Sang Buwaya!" called Kancil. "I have a message from King Suleiman! I have been asked to take a census and find out how many crocodiles are in this river. The King thinks there are about seven crocodiles here."

"No way!" shouted Sang Buwaya. "There are MANY MORE crocodiles in this river!"

"Well, line them up then, and I will count them," said Kancil.

So Sang Buwaya brought all of the crocodiles, and they lined up nose to tail until they stretched out clear across the river from one bank to another.

"Good!" called Kancil. "Now I will count the crocodiles. Do not move, any of you!"

Kancil jumped on the back of the first crocodile.

"One!"

He jumped on the back of the second crocodile.

"Two!"

"Three, four, five, six, five, four, three, five, six, seven, SEVEN! There are only SEVEN crocodiles in the river."

"That can't be right!" shouted Sang Buwaya. "Count them again, Kancil!"

"OK," said Kancil. "But first I must take a little rest. Stay right where you are, crocodiles."

Kancil sat down under the mango tree and ate until his tummy was very, very full of ripe, juicy mangoes.

"OK, Sang Buwaya. I am going to count crocodiles again," called Kancil.

He jumped onto the back of the first crocodile.

"One"

"Two, three, four, five, six, seven, eight, nine, ten, eleven, twelve. TWELVE!"

Kancil jumped onto the bank of the river.

"Twelve crocodiles! You were right, Sang Buwaya. There are more than seven! And by the way, thanks for making a bridge so I could cross the river and eat mangoes! Good-bye Sang Buwaya! I FOOLED YOU!"

Then Kancil Mouse Deer ran off into the forest.

I don't know if he ever tricked the crocodile again.

But I do know one thing: Sang Buwaya never did catch him!

KANCIL AND SANG HARIMAU

*K*ancil Mouse Deer is a very tiny animal. He has to be very careful because many larger animals would love to eat him for their dinner. But Kancil is so clever that he always finds a way to just trick those bigger animals.

One day when Kancil was passing through the forest, he came face to face with Sang Harimau, the Tiger!

"Selamat Pagi! Good day!" said Sang Harimau. "I think I see something tasty for my lunch!"

Kancil thought fast. He noticed a large snake lying beside the path.

"Sang Harimau, imagine meeting you today. I am just about to put on the belt of King Suleiman the Great." Kancil pointed at the huge snake.

"Only *I* am allowed to wear King Suleiman's belt, you know."

"Oh, Kancil! I want to wear King Suleiman's belt!" begged the Tiger. "Can I try it on? Just for a minute?"

"Well, if you insist." And Kancil stood back.

Sang Harimau picked up the long snake and wrapped it around his waist. But the snake began to squeeze. And squeeze.

"OOOFFFFF . . . ."

"Maybe I made a mistake," called Kancil as he ran off into the forest. "It looks like that is really a SNAKE! Good-bye, Sang Harimau. I FOOLED YOU!"

Another day Kancil met Sang Harimau again.

"Selamat Pagi!" said Sang Harimau. "It looks like I will have a good lunch today! Kancil for lunch!"

Kancil looked around. There was a split bamboo.

"Oh, I guess you will eat me for lunch, " said Kancil. "But first I need to play King Suleiman's flute. He has said that only *I* can play his special flute."

"Where is the flute of King Suleiman? I want to play it!" bawled the Tiger.

"Well, he said that I was the only one who could play it," replied Kancil. "But if you insist . . . . You put your tongue right here and blow."

Sang Harimau stuck his long tongue into the split in the bamboo, and Kancil let the bamboo flip back on that tongue.

"AAAYYYYY!"

"Oh, sorry, Sang Harimau. It looks like that is just a split bamboo. Guess you are trapped for a while. Good-bye, Sang Harimau! I FOOLED YOU!"

When Sang Harimau caught Kancil Mouse Deer the third time, he was very angry.

"All right, Kancil! I am really going to eat you now!"

Kancil looked around. There was a hornet's nest hanging from a tree right near the path.

"Oh well, then," said Kancil. "I guess you won't get to play King Suleiman's drum."

"Drum? Where is the drum of King Suleiman?"

"Why, right here," Kancil pointed. "But King Suleiman said that only *I* would be allowed to touch his special drum."

"Well, *I* am going to play it!" roared Sang Harimau. "And then I am going to EAT you!"

And Sang Harimau hit the hornet's nest with a strong WHACK of his paw!

"AAAYYYYY!"

"It looks like that was really a hornet's nest!" called Kancil as Sang Harimau ran off through the forest, pursued by stinging hornets.

"Good-bye, Sang Harimau! I FOOLED YOU!"

After that, whenever Sang Harimau saw Kancil coming down the forest path, he just turned and went the other direction!

KANCIL AND THE BIG HOLE

*O*ne day as Kancil Mouse Deer was passing through the forest, he stumbled and fell into a deep hole in the ground.

"Help! Help!" Kancil screamed for help.

He didn't know what to do. "How on earth can I get out of this deep hole?"

The hole was so deep that Kancil knew his animal friends wouldn't be able to pull him out.

He thought and thought.

Then Kancil saw a palm leaf lying on the floor of the hole. Some insects had eaten away parts of the leaf, and it looked sort of like Arabic letters.

"Aha!" Kancil had an idea.

He sat down and pretended to be reading from the leaf.

"Annnannnannnannnannnannnannn . . . AHHH! YES!"

"Annnannnannnannnannnannnannn . . . AHHH! YES!"

He read louder and louder.

"Annnannnannnannnannnannnannn . . . AHHH! YES!"

Gadja, the Elephant, peered over the edge of the hole.

"Kancil, what are you doing down there?"

"I am reading from the sacred palm leaf text of King Suleiman the Great. It says here that whoever comes down into the hole and listens to the reading will be blessed!"

"Oh, I want to listen to the sacred reading!" called Elephant.

And Gadjah Elephant JUMPED down into the hole!

Kancil looked at Elephant's back.

If he jumped onto Elephant's back, could he then jump out of the hole? Probably not.

So he kept on reading.

"Annnannnannnannnannnannnannn . . . AHHH! YES!"

"Annnannnannnannnannnannn . . . AHHH! YES!"

Kerbau, the Water Buffalo, peered over the edge of the hole.

"Kancil and Gadjah, what are you doing down there?"

"Kancil is reading from King Suleiman's sacred palm leaf text," called Gadjah Elephant. "Whoever comes down into the hole and listens to it will be blessed!"

"Well, stand aside! I am coming down!"

And Kerbau JUMPED down into the hole.

Kancil looked at the water buffalo. If he could get Kerbau to stand on the back of Gadjah Elephant and Kancil stood on the back of Kerbau, could he jump out of the hole? Probably not.

Kancil went on reading.

"Annnannnannnannnannnannnannn . . . AHHH! YES!"

"Annnannnannnannnannnannnannn . . . AHHH! YES!"

Just then Kambing, the Goat, came by. "What are you animals all doing down in that hole?"

"We are getting blessing!" called up Kerbau. "Kancil is reading from the sacred palm leaf text of King Suleiman the Great."

"Yes," added Kancil. "It says here, whoever comes down into the hole and listens to the sacred text will be blessed."

"I want to be blessed! I am coming down!"

And Kambing Goat JUMPED down into the hole.

Kancil looked at Kambing Goat. If Kambing Goat stood on the back of Kerbau and Kerbau stood on the back of Gadjah Elephant, could Kancil get on top and jump out of the hole? Probably not.

Kancil sighed and thought. Another plan!

Kancil began to read loudly.

"Annnannnannnannnannnannnannn . . . AHHH! YES!"

"Annnannnannnannnannnannnannn . . . AHHH! YES!"

"Oh! It says here, if anyone SNEEZES, they must be thrown OUT of the sacred hole! Don't sneeze, Gadjah! Don't sneeze, Kerbau! Don't sneeze, Kambing. We would have to throw you out!"

"I won't sneeze!" said Gadjah Elephant and rolled up his trunk.

"I won't sneeze!" said Kerbau and lowered his big head.

"I won't sneeze!" said Kambing Goat and held his breath.

"I won't sneeze!" said Kancil Mouse Deer. "Ahhh, ahhh, ahhh, CHOOO!"

"Kancil SNEEZED!" shouted all the animals.

"Throw him out of the hole! Throw him OUT!"

Elephant grabbed Kancil with his trunk and TOSSED him out of the hole!

"Thank you, friends!" called Kancil. "I wondered how I was going to get out of that hole!"

"Good-bye, Gadjah! Good-bye, Kerbau! Good-bye, Kambing! And by the way . . . I TRICKED YOU!"

KANCIL AND THE OTTER'S BABIES

The tiny mouse deer, Kancil, has a habit of rapping the ground with its little hind feet to call to other mouse deer during the mating season. It is said that it also does this to warn of danger.

One day Memerang Otter went down to the river to catch fish. She left her babies on the bank and asked Kancil Mouse Deer, then known as Sir Peace of the Forest, to watch them.

Now in those days Nabi Sleman (King Solomon) had been set by Allah to rule over all of the animals. Nabi Noh (Noah) had been put in charge of all the trees and plants. And Nabi Tuakal had discovered that Noah overlooked a few roots, so he decided to be in charge of those himself, and planted them on the trees! So the orchids and such which live only in the treetops, were under the charge of Nabi Tuakal.

After Otter swam away into the river, Kancil settled down on the riverbank, nibbling grass and keeping an eye on the baby otters. But suddenly he heard "Tap! Tap! Tap! Tap! Tap!" It was Woodpecker! He was drumming an alarm! Something was wrong in the forest!

At once Kancil began to pass the alarm along. He drummed with his little hind hoofs as hard as he could. "Rat-a-tat-a-tat-a-tat." Not watching what he was doing, the little mouse deer trampled right on the otter's nest. "Rat-a-tat-a-tat."

When Otter returned, she began to wail. "Mouse deer has trampled my babies! Mouse deer did not take care!"

Kancil was so sorry. He apologized. But it was too late.

Otter went right to King Solomon. "Kancil Mouse Deer has trampled my babies! I demand justice from you, King Solomon!"

"Well, let me hear about this matter," said King Solomon. "Just as no child was ever born without both a father and a mother, no judgment can be made without hearing both sides of the case. Bring Kancil Mouse Deer to me."

So court was held. All of the animals came. On one side of King Solomon's palace was the sea, full of all the sea fishes. On the other side was the river, full of the river fishes. On the land side were all of the forest animals, and in the trees were the birds and butterflies. Everyone had come to hear this case of Otter versus Kancil Mouse Deer.

Kancil bowed and said, "O King, what the Otter says is true. I did trample her babies. But Blato, the Woodpecker, had sounded the war alarm. I was only doing my duty to pass on the alarm. I accidentally trampled on Otter's babies while doing my duty. But the fault is with Woodpecker."

"Well, I will judge no one in his absence," said King Solomon. "Where is Woodpecker?"

Woodpecker came flying in. "King Solomon, I was only doing my duty in sounding the war alarm. I saw Tuntong, the River Turtle, and all of his kind leaving the river wearing their coats of armor. I had to sound the war alarm."

"Call Tuntong, the River Turtle here," said King Solomon. "What is this all about, Tuntong?"

"It was the FISH!" said Tuntong. "They came swimming up the river in battalions. The prawns had spikes between their eyes. The perches were wearing bright war sashes. The garfish were thrusting about with long pikes. I knew that war was at hand, so I led my people away from the river as fast as we could move."

"By the grace of Allah," said King Solomon, "this stream has many bends and turnings. Well, let's hear from the fish."

And when the prawns, and perch, and garfish had come forward, they said, "Oh King, you must understand. We were only fleeing from Otter. Otter was attacking from the rear and eating us! That is why we swam upstream in terror."

Then King Solomon turned to Memerang, the Otter. "Dear Otter, a great misfortune has occurred. But the fault seems to lie with you. It is not the arrow that is at fault, but he who draws the bow. If you had not harried the prawns, perch, and garfish, the River Turtles would not have fled the stream, and Woodpecker would not have raised a war alarm, and Kancil Mouse Deer would not have passed on the alarm, and your children would not have been harmed. Now, go in peace. The matter is unfortunate. But it is resolved. You may blame no one but yourself."

"Our judgment is delivered," proclaimed King Solomon. "All creatures must go home now, in peace."

Fables about Plants

Here we have three tales from the vegetable world! The first tells of a war among the many native species, with King Solomon trying to act as mediator. The second tale is an anecdote explaining how two villages learned to appreciate their own trees. The third tale reveals the origin of the use of cloves to freshen the breath.

A FIGHT AMONG THE VEGETABLES

A Malay tale collected in Pahang in 1899

*O*ne time Jagong the Corn plant started boasting, "If Rice died out, there would be no problem. Corn alone could feed all of the people. No one needs Rice anyway."

Then Dagun the Liana vine, said, "Oh, the same goes for me. I am MUCH more important than either Rice OR Corn." And Gadong the Forest Yam called out, "What about ME! I am much more important than ANY of you. People could easily live on yam and yam alone."

The vegetables began to argue and argue. And last they were brought to King Solomon.

"All three of you are right," said King Solomon. "Man *could* live on any of you alone. But Jagong, corn, you would be best. Especially if you worked with Kachang the Bean."

On hearing this, Dagun the Liana and Gadong the Forest Yam were furious. They went off to find a spike from the Fig Tree to spear Jagong. And Jagong, hearing of what they were up to, began to make himself poison arrows. Jagong shot one of his poison arrows right into Gadong! Thus to this day the Jungle Yam can be used to make poison arrows, and it must be washed many times to get all the poison out before it can be eaten. In return, Gadong Yam stabbed Jagong Maize over and over. So today corn cobs are perforated with holes. Then Jagong grabbed a pointed shoot and stabbed Dagun Liana. And thus the fight continued.

The quarrel was now taken to the Prophet Elias. "This quarrel is too much for me," said the Prophet Elias. "You will have to go back to King Solomon."

King Solomon was frustrated with these quarreling vegetables. "Well, just let them fight it out," he said. "Eventually their anger will be satisfied."

So a raging battle among the vegetables began. For twice times seven days they fought.

Mata Lémbu, the Ox-Eye Tree, stood close and watched the battle. His bark is still scratched where he was cut. But the Perachak Bush was terrified and stood a long way off and got on tiptoe to see what was happening. To this day it grows long and lanky.

Meanwhile the sedge And'ram was so frightened that it ran and hid in the river, where it still lives.

When twice time seven days had passed, King Solomon called a halt to the fighting.

"That is enough! You vegetables will never get along together. I will just have to separate you." So he put a space between them all. Gadong the Forest Yam was sent to sit in the ground on one side. Dagun the Liana was told to go lie down in a different place. And Jagong the corn plant was sent to stand with Kachang the Bean in another field. And thus the order of the vegetables was established that continues to this day.

GELUGUR AND JELUTUNG

A folktale from Penang

*T*here was once a village called Kampung Gelugur. The village was surrounded by *gelugur* trees. These trees bore a lot of fruit. But the villagers had no use for the fruit. So the ripe fruit fell from the trees and piled up on the ground, rotted, and made a smelly mess. At last the villagers decided to just cut the trees down.

One tree they did prize, however, was the *jelutung* tree. But this could be found only in the jungle and was hard to locate. They needed to find *jelutung* trees so they could use the *jelutung* resin to burn in their lamps. And they also used the resin to season their food.

Now some distance away there was another village. This village was called Kampung Jelutung. It was surrounded by *jelutung* trees! But no one there had any use for them. They decided to cut them down. The tree they prized was the *gelugur* tree. They dried the fruit and used it in their cooking. But the *gelugur* trees were deep in the jungle and hard to find.

Fortunately a man from Kampung Jelutung happened to be traveling past Kampung Gelugur just as the villagers began to chop down their *gelugur* trees.

"What are you doing?" The Kampung Jelutung man was horrified. "Why would you cut down a perfectly good *gelugur* tree?"

"Oh, these trees are worthless," replied one of the men. "They just make a mess with their rotten fruit. We are going to get rid of them."

"But the fruit of the *gelugur* tree is DELICIOUS! You just have to know how to prepare it!" said the Jelutung man. "Don't cut your trees down! Send one of your women home with me and my wife will show her how to prepare delicious dishes with the *gelugur* fruit."

So the woman and her friends from Kampung Gelugur traveled to Kampung Jelutung. The people there were just preparing to chop down their *jelutung* trees.

"Stop! What are you doing?" cried the Kampung Gelugur woman.

"Oh, these *jelutung* trees are worthless. We are just getting rid of them."

"Worthless? These trees are VERY valuable. Don't you know how to get resin from these trees? It is perfect to burn in lamps. And it also is great to add flavor to certain dishes. Please don't cut down these valuable trees!"

The villagers looked at each other. "This is amazing news. We shouldn't cut down our trees after all!"

So the two villages kept their trees. The folks of Kampung Gelugur learned to love the taste of their delicious *gelugur* fruit. And the folks of Kampung Jelutung learned to use the resin of their *jelutung* trees in their lamps and to season their food with the resin, too.

The two villages began to trade with each other. "How about a basket of *gelugur* fruit for a kilo of *jelutung* resin?" "Good deal!"

And so the trees were saved and new friendships were made.

CLOVES FOR THE BREATH

A folktale from Johore

*T*here was once a land where everyone had bad breath. This was a real problem. No one wanted to talk to anyone else. Everyone kept their distance. The King had no idea what to do for his people.

One day when the princess and her friends were playing in the garden, a *murai* bird landed near them. "Cheep! Cheep!" The bird seemed to be calling to the princess. She went closer. The bird began to hop from bush to bush. "Cheep! Cheep!" It landed on a bush covered with little flowers. The bird began to peck at the flowers and look up at the princess. She watched it but didn't seem to understand. So the bird selected a flower, broke it off, and flew to drop it in her hand. The princess smiled and smelled the flower. Its scent was unusual and delighted her. She put the little flower in her mouth and tasted it. Mmmm! What a sweet smell!

The princess picked a few more of the blossoms and chewed them, then she shared some with her friends. "Aaaaahhhh!" Their breath became sweet and fresh!

"Father! Look what the *murai* bird showed us!"

The King was thrilled with this discovery. He ordered his subjects to all plant this bush, and to chew its blossoms and seeds every day. From then on this kingdom was known for the sweet breath of its inhabitants.

The bush, *bunga cengkih*, was the plant we know today as the clove. And people all over the world still chew this to freshen their breath.

Humorous Malay Tales:
Pak Pandir and Other Foolish Fellows

    Tales of foolish wise men are told throughout the Muslim world. In Egypt stories are told of Goha. In Turkey it is Nasruddin Hodja. In Iran the tales are told of the Mullah. And here in Malaysia it is Pak Pandir, or sometimes his friend Pak Kadok and others. Many short, humorous tales are told about these fellows. Sometimes they pretend to be foolish but are really wise; sometimes they are just plain foolish. Here are a few tales about Pak Pandir.

LENDING THE WATER BUFFALO

*O*ne day Pak Pandir's friend came to ask if he could borrow Pak Pandir's water buffalo. "Oh, I am so sorry," replied Pak Pandir. "But my water buffalo is not here right now. I cannot loan him to you today."

Just then the water buffalo, who was standing out behind the house, let out a loud bellow.

"There! I hear him! The water buffalo IS here!" cried his friend. But Pak Pandir drew himself up and looked in scorn at his friend.

"What? Do you mean that you will take the word of a simple water buffalo over MINE?" Pak Pandir was indignant.

"Then I certainly cannot loan anything to such a friend."

And Pak Pandir went into the house and closed the door.

PAK PANDIR AND PAK KADOK GO SHOPPING

*A*ctually, Pak Pandir wasn't the only foolish fellow in Malayan folklore. His friend Pak Kadok was just as bad.

One day Pak Pandir's wife sent him to town to buy a buffalo. But Pak Pandir didn't seem to know what she wanted. "You know," she shouted, "a grass eater!"

"Oh, yes. Okay. How shall I get the 'grass eater' home?"

"Just tie a rope around it and lead it," muttered his disgruntled wife.

Pak Pandir took some money and went off for town. On the way he saw a man cutting grass with a scythe. "What on earth is that?" asked Pak Pandir.

"Oh, that's my grass eater," said the man. "I call it that because it cuts my grass."

"Why, that is just what I am looking for!" exclaimed Pak Pandir. "Will you sell it?"

So he gave the man a large sum of money, tied a rope to the scythe, and went off dragging his "grass eater" behind him.

Soon he met his good friend Pak Kadok. Pak Kadok had just come from town, where he had bought a packet of salt for his wife. He had the salt in his pocket.

"Let's take a shortcut across the river," said Pak Pandir. "We will be home in no time at all."

"But how can we cross the river?" wondered Pak Kadok.

Pak Pandir looked around. There was a line of ants riding down the river on top of a little log.

"If the ants can ride a log across the river, so can we."

So the two men straddled a little log and started rowing out into the river. But just before they reached the opposite shore, the log rolled over. They were dumped into the water.

The foolish pair waded ashore, sopping wet. There was nothing to do but lie down in the sun to dry off. Soon the two were fast asleep.

In a tree over their heads two little monkeys were playing. One monkey dropped a nut onto Pak Kadok's head.

"Hey! Don't hit me, Pak Pandir!"

"I didn't hit you. Go back to sleep."

Now the second monkey dropped a nut on Pak Pandir's head.

"Stop that, Pak Kadok! You have no reason to hit me!"

"I didn't hit you. Go back to sleep."

Then the two monkeys looked at each other. They each held out a nut, and dropped them onto the two sleeping men at the same time.

"Stop that!"

"YOU stop that!"

The two started hitting each other and were into a noisy fight when they suddenly heard the monkeys chattering away at them.

"So it was you monkeys! Well, you managed to start a fight, that is for sure."

Pak Pandir and Pak Kadok were dried off by now. So they went on home.

Pak Pandir's wife was waiting for him.

"Where is the Buffalo?"

"Oh, I brought you a good 'grass eater.' Here it is!"

He pulled on the rope and dragged in the scythe.

"This is not a Buffalo! Where is my money?"

"Oh, I gave it to the man who sold me the great 'grass eater'."

"You foolish man!" And his wife chased Pak Pandir out of the house.

Meanwhile Pak Kadok had reached his home.

"Where is the salt I sent you to buy?" demanded his wife.

"It is right here in my pocket." And he handed her the packet that had contained the salt.

Of course the salt was all gone, as it had dissolved when he fell into the water.

"You foolish man!" His wife chased him out of the house.

Pak Pandir and Pak Kadok met on the road. "Nothing I do pleases my wife," said Pak Pandir. "Nothing I do pleases my wife, either," said Pak Kadok. So the two men walked off down the road together. Probably to get into more foolishness.

PAK PANDIR AND THE GIANT GERGASI

Retold by Singapore storyteller Kamini Ramachandran

*O*ne day Mak Andam, Pak Pandir's wife, decided to have a *kenduri* party and wanted to invite the Tok Imam, head of the village mosque. She sent her husband, dear old Pak Pandir, to go and personally invite Tok Imam. But before she sent him off, Mak Andam warned him that there were two roads leading out of the village. "Remember," she said, "the road on the right leads to Tok Imam's house, but the road on the left leads to Tok Gergasi, the GIANT!"

Pak Pandir went off, singing, "Right Tok Imam, Left Tok Gergasi, home *kenduri*." But soon he was confused and was singing, "Right Tok Gergasi, Left Tok Imam, home *kenduri*." By the time he came to the fork in the road, he was completely befuddled, and of course he took the wrong road!

Pak Pandir walked and walked for a very long time, but Tok Imam's house was nowhere in sight! The surroundings had become very quiet and still, no birds chirping, no insects buzzing, no monkeys chattering.

There Pak Pandir saw a big house. He was impressed with the Imam's home! He hadn't realized the Imam was so wealthy that he could afford such a beautiful and large home. Then there stood the Giant Gergasi. Yuck! Gergasi's hair was matted, he was covered with the skin of some dead animal, and was wearing human bones strung around his neck! And the filthy giant smelled just terrible! "What good luck for Gergasi!" boomed his thunderous voice. "My LUNCH has arrived!"

"Oh dear!" Pak Pandir had to think quickly. "But Gergasi, I have come to invite you to our *kenduri* party. My wife invites you to come eat. She is preparing *lauk kerbau* (buffalo curry), *gulai pucuk ubi* (young tapioca shoots in gravy), *ayam goreng* (fried chicken), *ikan panggang* (grilled fish), *nasi kuning* (yellow rice), and *air limau manis* (fresh sweet lime juice). By this time Gergasi was drooling in anticipation. "Why thank you, Pak Pandir! I would be happy to come to your wife's feast!"

So Pak Pandir arrived home, with the Giant Gergasi clumping along behind.

Mak Andam was shocked to see that her husband had brought home a giant! What could she do? Mak Andam brought out the food and began to serve the gross Gergasi.

Gergasi ate *lauk kerbau* (buffalo curry). Until it was all gone.

Gergasi ate *gulai pucuk ubi* (young tapioca shoots in gravy). Until it was all gone.

Gergasi ate *ayam goreng* (fried chicken). Until it was all gone.

Gergasi ate *ikan panggang* (grilled fish). Until it was all gone.

Then he finished off the *nasi kuning* (yellow rice), and sloshed down the *limau manis* (fresh sweet lime juice).

"MORE FOOD!" roared Gergasi. "More food, or I will eat YOU!"

Pak Pandir and Mak Andam looked at each other. "Run for your life!"

The two took off running toward the river as fast as they could go. But right behind them came the angry Gergasi. The earth was shaking under his feet.

Fortunately there was a *pirahu* on the river bank. Pak Pandir and Mak Andam jumped into the little boat and quickly rowed across the river.

But here came Gergasi thundering up to the river bank.

"Too late, Gergasi!" shouted Mak Andam. "We are already on the other side of the river!"

"Oh, but how can I reach you then?" called Gergasi.

Mak Andam knew that Gergasi was not very bright. "By rowing over on a *pirahu,* of course."

"But I don't have a *pirahu!*"

"Then go back to our house and bring the *tempayan* cooking pot."

Gergasi ran back to the house and was quickly back. carrying the *tempayan*.

"Tell me then, now what do I do to catch you?"

"Get inside the *tempayan* and row with your hands, of course!"

"Like this?" Gergasi climbed into the pot and started paddling himself into the river.

"That's the way!" called Mak Andam. "Now you need to hit the *tempayan* on its sides really hard."

"Like this?" Gergasi began to bang on the sides of the *tempayan*.

"No, hit it harder! Then it will bring you right where you need to go."

So Gergasi gave the *tempayan* one huge blow! And the pot broke right in two. Which meant that Gergasi went indeed right where he needed to go . . . right to the bottom of the river.

PART 3

Tales from the Ethnic Peoples of Borneo

Tales from Sabah

On the end of Borneo Island nearest the Philippines lies the Malaysian state of Sabah. Coastal areas were settled by Malay, but the interior remained the home of indigenous Bornean people. Today roads have opened up much of Sabah and a modern lifestyle is common. But many still remember the stories of their grandparents. Sabah is home to the Kadazan, Dusun, Murut, Sungai, and other groups. The Kadazandusun Language Foundation devotes itself to collecting and preserving folktales from the elders. This section draws some tales from their work. Other tales were told to this author during visits to Sabah in 1996, 2003, and 2006.

THE TERRIBLE KARAMBAU

A Kadazandusun folktale; as told by Yunis Rojiin Gabu, heard from her grandmother, Gunih Rampasan of Kampong Togop Tamparuli, Sabah

A little boy was sent out to get firewood by his mother. There was Bubut Bird tangled up in a vine. The boy untangled it.

"Thank you," said Bubut Bird and flew away.

Here was Ikus Mouse caught by a snake. The boy grabbed a stick and beat off the snake and drove it away.

"Thank you," said Ikus Mouse.

The boy continued on into the forest, looking for firewood.

Suddenly there was a Giant Karambau! The big, hairy, stinky creature grabbed the little boy and carried him home to its cave.

There it handed the *anak-anak* (child) over to his wife.

"Here! Fatten this skinny kid up! We are going to have *anak-anak* stew!"

The little boy tried hard not to eat enough to get fat. But the Giant Wife kept pushing food at him.

When she was not looking, the boy began trying to dig an escape route around the huge stone that the giant Karambau had rolled across the cave entrance.

He worked quietly and industriously. Eventually he made a tiny hole.

It was just big enough to see through to the outside.

Immediately another VERY tiny eye peered back at him. It was the little mouse!

Ikus Mouse had followed the boy and had been watching, hoping for a way to rescue him.

"Do you need help?" called the little mouse.

"Yes! I really do need help," whispered the boy.

"Wait here. I will get help."

The little mouse scurried away. He soon returned with Bubut Bird.

"We can help." said the mouse. "You keep digging on your side. We will start digging on our side. We will get you out."

And Ikus Mouse began to dig.

"Kukut-kukutai Ikus . . . kut! kut!

Kukut-kukutai Ikus . . . kut! kut!"

And while the mouse dug, the Bubut Bird swept the dirt away with its wings.

"Kurub-kurubai Ubut . . . krub! krub!

Kurub-kurubai Ubut . . . krub! krub!"

"Hey! What is that noise I hear?" called the Giant Wife.

"Oh, it is just me crunching on my bones." said the little boy.

"Oh, good. Keep eating," replied the Giant Wife.

Soon the hole was big enough for the boy to begin pushing bits of food through the hole. Quickly the mouse passed them on to Bubut Bird, who carried them away and hid them. The Giant Wife thought the boy was finally beginning to eat well.

"He will be fat in no time at this rate," she thought.

Every day the mouse helped the boy dig.

"Kukut-kukutai Ikus . . . kut! kut!

Kukut-kukutai Ikus . . . kut! kut!"

"Kurub-kurubai Ubut . . . krub! krub!

Kurub-kurubai Ubut . . . krub! krub!"

"Hey! What's that noise I hear?"

"Oh it is just me, scraping my dish."

"He will soon be fat enough to eat," thought the Giant's wife.

After a while the hole was big enough for the boy to put his arm through.

"Kukut-kukutai Ikus . . . kut! kut!

Kukut-kukutai Ikus . . . kut! kut!"

"Kurub-kurubai Ubut . . . krub! krub!

Kurub-kurubai Ubut . . . krub! krub!"

After another long while, the hole was big enough for the boy to put his head through.

"Kukut-kukutai Ikus . . . kut! kut!

Kukut-kukutai Ikus . . . kut! kut!"

"Kurub-kurubai Ubut . . . krub! krub!

Kurub-kurubai Ubut . . . krub! krub!"

After another really long while, the hole was big enough for the boy to put his whole body through! With one big PUSH, the boy squeezed through the hole. He was free!

"Crunch! Crunch! Crunch!" The boy heard the Giant's footsteps. He was coming home!

"Quick!" squeaked Ikus Mouse. "This way!"

"Hurry!" cried Bubut Bird. "Follow us!"

Ikus Mouse scurried through the forest, showing the boy the way.

Bubut Bird flew ahead, spying out the trail.

Home ran the boy. How glad his mother was to see him.

And do you know, she never sent him so deep into the forest to look for firewood again.

No, no. She kept him safe, close to home.

About this story: *This story was told to Margaret Read MacDonald and Jen and Nat Whitman in a library van en route to Kota Kinabalu , coming home from a day of storytelling performances. Yunis Rojiin, our host librarian, suddenly said, "The stories you folks told remind me of stories my grandmother used to tell." And she told us this wonderful story. Copyright Yunis Rojiin Gabu, 2003.*

THE ROLLING RED-EYED HEAD

A Kadazandusun folktale; as told by Yunis Rojiin Gabu, heard from her grandmother, Gunih Rampasan of Kampong Togop Tamparuli, Sabah

*T*here was once an impatient boy. He could never wait for anything.

If the rice was cooking, he wanted it NOW.

If the yams were cooking, he wanted them NOW. And when it came to durian fruit, he could never wait for the fruit to ripen properly and drop delicious from the tree.

No. He wanted it NOW.

One day the boy just couldn't wait any longer for the durian fruit to ripen.

Grabbing a long stick, he began to knock at the fruit in the tree.

Whack! Whack! Whack!

And suddenly PLOP!

A huge durian dropped right beside him.

Success!

But the boy didn't have time to gloat over his clever picking of the fruit.

Because the Durian split open . . . and a big head with red, red eyes jumped out!

"AAAAHHHH!" The boy screamed and ran.

But the red-eyed head JUMPED!

It LUNGED right at the boy!

After him it came. "TUNG! TUNG! TUNG!" That angry head bounced along after the boy. "Help me! Help me!" The boy was running and screaming for help.

There was a yam plant.

"I'll help you little boy. Hide behind me," said the yam plant.

So the boy hid behind the yam plant.

UP came the red-eyed head.

The yam moved its leaves this way and that, trying to protect the boy.

"You can move all you want, yam plant. But you can't stop me from getting that mean little boy who pulled me from my tree!"

And the red-eyed head LUNGED at the yam plant, laughing all the while.

"Run!" called the yam plant. "I can't hold the red-eyed head back much longer. RUN!"

Little Boy ran on. "Help me! Help me!" The little boy ran as hard as he could, but . . .

"TUNG! TUNG! TUNG!" The red-eyed head could bounce just as fast.

"I can save you, Little Boy!" called the tapioca plant. "Come hide by me."

Quickly the boy hid behind the tapioca plant.

But the red-eyed head just laughed.

"You think you can protect that little boy? Just watch me jump right through you, Tapioca!" And the red-eyed head LUNGED at the tapioca plant.

"You'd better RUN!" called the tapioca. "I can't protect you much longer!"

"Help! Help!" The little boy ran on.

"TUNG! TUNG! TUNG!" The red-eyed head jumped after him.

"Bitter Melon! Bitter Melon! Can you save me?"

"Hide behind me, Little Boy. I will save you."

But UP came the red-eyed head. "Bitter Melon, you can't save that mean little boy. I can roll right through you!"

And the red-eyed head LUNGED at Bitter Melon.

"Run!" moaned Bitter Melon. "I can't hold the red-eyed head back much longer!"

ON ran Little Boy.

"TUNG! TUNG! TUNG!" ON came the red-eyed head.

"Papaya! Papaya! Please help me! Red-eyed Head is after me!"

"Quick, get behind me. I will protect you."

Little Boy got behind Papaya.

But Papaya's trunk is very skinny.

Red-eyed Head could easily see him there.

"I can get you now, you mean little boy!"

And the red-eyed head LUNGED. Red-eyed Head struck Papaya, and papayas fell to the ground.

"RUN!" called Papaya. "I can't protect you!"

On ran Little Boy.

"TUNG! TUNG! TUNG!" The red-eyed head was right after him.

"Banana Tree! Banana Tree! Please help me! Red-eyed Head is right behind me!"

"Just stand behind me, Little Boy. I will protect you."

Banana tree began to sway this way and that. For a moment Red-eyed Head was confused. What had happened to Little Boy?

Then it spied him.

"Banana Tree, you can sway all you want. You can't keep me away from that mean little boy."

And the red-eyed head LUNGED at Banana Tree.

"RUN!" called Banana Tree. "I can't save you!"

Little Boy ran.

"TUNG! TUNG! TUNG!" Red-Eyed Head bounced closer and closer.

"Sago Tree! Sago Tree! Help me!"

"Get behind my trunk. I will save you!" said Sago Tree. "I have prickles!"

"You don't fool ME!" called the red-eyed head. " I SEE you there!"

Red-eyed Head LUNGED! The prickles couldn't stop him.

"RUN!" called Sago. "I can't save you after all!"

Little Boy ran and ran.

"TUNG! TUNG! TUNG!" came the bouncing red-eyed head.

Little Boy had reached the edge of the river. There was only one last plant here to save him, just the bamboo clump.

"Bamboo! Bamboo! You have GOT to save me. Red-eyed Head is after me!"

Bamboo bent over and looked at Little Boy.

"And just WHY is Red-eyed Head after you?"

"I made a mistake. I made a BAD mistake. I didn't wait for Durian to get ripe. I knocked Durian down with a stick. Red-eyed Head jumped out of Durian and is after me. Oh, PLEASE hide me! I promise I won't ever do it again!"

"I can hide you," said Bamboo. "And I can stop Red-eyed Head. But I do not want to hear that you have been acting impatiently like that ever again!"

Little Boy hid behind Bamboo Clump.

Red-eyed Head bounced up.

"Where is that little boy? He had to come this way. Where is he?"

Bamboo just sneered at Red-eyed Head.

"You want Little Boy? Well, he is inside my clump here. Just jump right in and get him."

Then Bamboo Clump split itself open. Suddenly there were many sharp bamboo slivers sticking out from the broken bamboo edges. Everywhere it was sharp, sharp.

And the furious Red-eyed Head LUNGED!

But "AAAHHHH!" Red-eyed Head was stuck on those sharp, sharp bamboo slivers.

And that was the end of Red-eyed Head.

"Thank you, thank you, Bamboo!" said Little Boy. And he went home much reformed.

After that, if the rice was cooking, Little Boy would sit patiently.

"I can wait. No problem."

If the yams were slow in cooking, Little Boy would sit patiently.

"I can wait. No problem."

And when the durian fruit was ripening, Little Boy would watch the tree patiently.

"I can wait. And wait. And wait . . . . No problem."

About this story: *Another tale told to Margaret Read MacDonald and Jen and Nat Whitman by librarian Yunis Rojiin. See note for "The Terrible Karambau" on page 85. Copyright Yunis Rojiin Gabu, 2003.*

THE GIRL WHO WAS KIDNAPPED BY AN ORANGUTAN

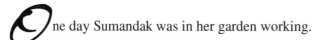

A Kadazandusun folktale; as told by Yunis Rojiin Gabu, heard from her grandmother, Gunih Rampasan of Kampong Togop Tamparuli, Sabah

*O*ne day Sumandak was in her garden working.

Suddenly a HUGE Orangutan leapt out of the jungle, grabbed Sumandak, and carried her off. Though she kicked and screamed, she could not break loose. The Orangutan carried her deep into the jungle and up a tall tree. There he kept her in his tree. She could not get down from this tall perch. There were no long vines that she could hang on to, no way to climb down.

But the Orangutan did not hurt Sumandak. In fact, he was in love with her!

"You are SO beautiful," said the Orangutan. "You will be very happy here as my wife. In seven days my relatives will come and we will have the wedding."

"How can I marry an Orangutan?" thought Sumandak. "But how can I get down from here? This tree is too tall. If I jump I will die. It is hopeless." She could see that there were no vines at all near the top of the tree, nothing to hold onto to lower herself to the ground.

The next day the Orangutan brought her food. She ate it. But she kept the skins and did not throw them out.

The Orangutan was very messy. There were vines and twigs sticking into his hair all over. Suddenly the girl had an idea! If she could pull out some of the Orangutan's long hair, perhaps she could weave a rope!

"Dear Orangutan, you are SO messy. Let me help you clean yourself up."

"Am I messy? I didn't know that." The Orangutan felt very embarrassed. He wanted to make a good impression on Sumandak. He was bringing her the best fruits every night. He really wanted her to like him.

"I can help. Just sit down here and I will take away all those vines and twigs sticking out."

So the Orangutan sat quietly and Sumandak began to groom him. Slowly she combed his hair. And she put aside all of the twigs and vines she removed. She did not throw anything away.

The Orangutan soon fell fast asleep as she combed his fur. When he was sleeping deeply, Sumandak pulled out a handful of fur. "Ouch! What was that?"

"Dear Orangutan, did you feel that? I was just tickling you a bit."

"OK." The Orangutan went back to sleep.

Next day Sumandak did the same thing.

"Come sit here, dear Orangutan. I will clean you up a bit."

And when he was sleeping, "Ouch! What was that?"

"Oh, silly Orangutan. Don't you like it when I tickle you a little?"

And so, day by day, Sumandak was able to save quite a pile of Orangutan fur. And while he slept, she began to weave a rope, which she hid from the Orangutan.

By the third day she had a long rope. When the Orangutan was gone out foraging for food, she lowered the rope from the treetop. It was not long enough.

But the fourth day the rope was getting longer. But when she tested it, it was not long enough yet.

On the fifth day, when the Orangutan came home in the evening he said, "I think I am handsome enough now. You won't need to clean my fur anymore. Look how good I look. And my fur is feeling very light. I don't want you to pull on it anymore."

"Your face could still use a little help," said the girl. "I think if I trimmed your hairy face a bit you would look more handsome yet."

"Well, alright." And the Orangutan let her trim his face.

So by the sixth day the rope was very long. As soon as the Orangutan left the tree, the girl dropped the rope and prepared to climb down, but it was still not long enough. The situation was becoming desperate. On the seventh day the Orangutan's relatives would arrive for the wedding. If she didn't escape before then, it would be too late.

That night when the Orangutan arrived home, he was very excited. "Tomorrow is our wedding, girl! My relatives will come and you will become my bride!"

"Then I must clean you up some more," said Sumandak.

"No, I don't think so. I am already handsome enough," said the Orangutan. "Besides, if you trim anymore of my hair, I will be too chilly."

"You do look handsome now," said Sumandak. "But you know we forgot to trim your tail. I think I should just trim a bit there."

So the Orangutan let her trim some hair from his tail.

After awhile the Orangutan fell asleep. Sumandak could see that she needed just a little more hair to finish her rope. So she began to pull really hard at the last hairs on his tail.

"What are you doing?!"

"Oh, dear Orangutan, there is a bad stain here, I have to scrub really hard to get it out. You want to look so beautiful tomorrow when your family comes. Just let me finish cleaning you up."

The Orangutan thought she was really trying to make him beautiful. He did not suspect one thing. So he fell back asleep.

Quietly the girl lowered the rope from the treetop. Down and down it went; far below she could see that the rope was long enough!

Quickly she climbed down the rope and ran away home through the forest.

In the morning the Orangutan woke up. "Today is my wedding day! My relatives will come soon!"

But alas, Sumandak was gone. He had been tricked!

About this story: When Yunis told this story, she said, "I didn't like the ending, because Grandma said just 'He had been tricked!' There was no more elaboration. But it got me thinking." Perhaps you can make up your own ending to the story. What did the Orangutan do, now that his human bride had escaped?

This was told to me at the Sabah State Library in Kota Kinabalu in August 2006 during a break in our storytelling workshop. Yunis had been thinking about more stories from her grandmother that she could tell me. She had shared "The Rolling Red-eyed Head" and "The Terrible Karambau" with my daughter and son-in-law and me during our 2003 storytelling tour, and I had typed them up and given her copies. She knew that I would like to hear more stories, so she had a headful ready to share with me. Copyright Yunis Rojin Gabu, 2006.

THE FAIRY BRIDE

A Kadazandusun folktale; as told by Yunis Rojiin Gabu, heard from her grandmother, Gunih Rampasan of Kampong Togop Tamparuli, Sabah

*A*nak-wagu was a farmer. Her was very handsome, but also very shy. It seemed he could not find a wife. Someone else always got to the beautiful girl first.

One day Anak-wagu noticed that a large pumpkin seemed to have sprung up overnight. Surprised, he walked over to the pumpkin and patted its surface. It seemed as if some strong force were drawing him toward that pumpkin. No sooner had he touched the pumpkin, than it fell open and there stood a beautiful young maiden! Of course they fell in love immediately; that is the way of these stories. And they were married and lived happily.

But before she agreed to marry him, the maiden, Sumandak, told Anak-wagu, "Whatever you do, you must never tell anyone where you found me. Do you promise this one thing?"

So Anak-wagu promised that he would never, under any circumstances, reveal where he had found his wife. The couple lived happily for some time, and a beautiful baby boy was born to them.

But the village people would not let Anak-wagu alone. How could this shy man have married such a beautiful woman? Where on earth did she come from? They bothered him daily with questions about this. He refused to say anything.

But at last Anak-wagu could not take the questioning any longer. His best friend waited for a time when Anak-wagu was exhausted, choosing his moment carefully.

"Surely you can tell me your secret? Where on earth did you find this beautiful wife? I'd love to find a woman like that for myself."

"If you want a wife like that, find a pumpkin and cut it," sighed Anak-wagu at last. And at once he realized he should not have spoken.

But it was too late. When Anak-wagu reached home, he saw his wife on the veranda embracing their little boy. He knew what he had done and he regretted it so much. But a

---

word of promise is a word of promise. "You did not keep your word, Anak-wagu," said Sumandak. "I cannot stay with you anymore. But whatever happens, please take care of our son."

Anak-wagu tried to stop her, but is was no use. She seemed pulled by some unseen force. She walked away from him as if drawn by a powerful magnet. She turned back but once. "If you want to ever see me again, Anak-wagu, you must reach that farthest hill before sunrise tomorrow." And so saying, she vanished into the forest. The hill to which she had pointed was at least two days' journey away. But Anak-wagu could not let her go. Bundling the boy onto his back, he took food and water and started out, following the way she had gone.

It was getting dark already. Soon it was so dark he could not see where he was stepping. But Anak-wagu struggled on. If he fell, he got up. He pushed aside branches and climbed over logs; he was determined to reach the far off hill before sunrise and reclaim his wife. It was, of course, impossible. The hill was much too far away. And stumbling, he fell into a ravine; the baby broke loose from his back and went tumbling down the hillside. "My son!" Then with horror he saw a giant python reach out and coil itself around the boy. And down the hill rolled the python, with the boy wrapped in its coils. What should he do? To follow the python was foolish. The boy would already be dead by the time he reached it. And he was losing precious time. He needed to climb back up to the trail and hurry on toward the mountain. But just then something pricked him. He thought it was a mosquito and started to swat at it, then he realized it was a firefly. And looking at the little firefly, he remembered the last words of his wife. "Take care of our son." He had to at least try to rescue the boy.

So down the hill he plunged, following the rolling python. Farther and farther, all night he plunged on in the dark. Now and then he would stop, exhausted, and think, "This is a lost cause. I should climb back to the path. I am losing too much time. I will never reach my wife by sunrise." But always the little firefly would prick him. And he would realize, "No. I must take care of my child."

The entire night passed in this way. Struggling on and on following the rolling python, never quite able to reach his child. The darkness began to fade, the firefly's little light was growing dimmer and dimmer, dark would break soon. It was too late now, he would never reach the distant hill before sunrise. He would never see his wife again.

Then suddenly the python rolled out into a valley! The land leveled off. The python stopped. It uncoiled itself and moved away back into the forest. The baby sat unhurt on the grass.

And on the other side of the valley Anak-wagu saw the distant mountain he had been told to reach. The sun was just starting to rise! But he was here! And there was his wife, walking slowly up the hill, toward a group of beautiful glowing maidens. It was too late!

"Sumandak!" Anak-wagu called out to her.

But she did not turn.

"Sumandak!"

Still she moved on toward the approaching maidens. If she reached them, he knew they would take her away with them forever.

"Sumandak!"

And then he felt the tiny firefly pricking and pricking him. He looked down at the tiny creature, and he realized, he had not even picked up the little boy. "Take care of our son," she had said.

Anak-wagu ran and scooped the child up in his arms. Then that boy let out such a cry! Such a loud cry Anak-wagu had never heard before!

At once Sumandak stopped in her tracks. She turned. And the maidens vanished.

Sumandak ran back down the hill to embrace her child and her husband. And as the sun rose, a happy family started the long trek back to their home.

About this story: The maiden's name, Sumandak, is simply the Kadazan name for "girl." Anak-wagu means young man. Yunis Rojiin, who told me this story in 2006, talked about the difficult decision Anak-wagu had to make, choosing between his wife and his son. See note for "The Girl who Was Kidnapped by an Orangutan" on page 92. Copyright Yunis Rojin Gabu, 2006.

STEALING FRUIT:
TWO DUSUN PUZZLE TALES

A boy came along with a *sisit* pole for picking fruit. (This is a long pole with a basket cup at the top. You pick fruit by putting the basket under the hanging fruit and dislodging it into the basket.)

"Get out of here," said the man who owned the fruit tree. "You cannot pick fruit from my tree."

"Oh, I understand that," said the boy. "I'm just wondering if my *sisit* pole is long enough. Maybe I should get a better one. Yours looks longer. Could I measure mine against yours?"

"Sure. No problem," said the owner of the fruit tree. So he stopped picking his fruit and held his pole up beside that of the boy to measure them.

The boy wiggled around with his pole and measured and measured. After a while he said. "Oh, yours is definitely longer." And he tossed his pole into the bushes.

Later the boy took his pole home and ate the fruit he had stolen. How did he steal the fruit?

Answer: While he pretended to measure his pole against that of the tree's owner, he was actually poking around in the branches and getting fruit to fall into the cup of his *sisit.*

Moral: You must know how to set about a thing if you want to do it.

Next day the boy found a tree whose fruit hung down against the side of a mountain. "Oh, this is easy. I will climb the mountain and get over into the top of the tree easily. Then I can pick all the fruit I want." So the boy did this. As he picked the fruit, he threw it down to the ground, planning to gather it later. But after he had picked all of the fruit from the branches, the boughs, which had been hanging down against the hillside heavy with fruit, now sprang up into the air, and the boy couldn't get down again.

Just then the tree's owner came by. "Aha! You thought you were clever, didn't you? Now how will you get down? Well, clever boy, I will just leave the fruit right here under the tree. If you can get down the same way you got up, you can have it. But I think you will still be there tonight when I come back."

But when the man returned that night, the boy and the fruit were gone. How did the boy get down from the tree?

Answer: The boy fastened together the leaves on the branches near the hillside to make little cups. When the afternoon rains came, they filled the cups with water, the weight pulled the branches back down, and the boy was able to climb off onto the hillside again.

Moral: Ingenuity overcomes difficulties.

THE PYTHON HUSBAND

A Sungai tale from Sabah; retold and performed by Margaret Read MacDonald

A girl and her mother were awakened one night by the chickens squawking under their house. They hurried to look down from the balcony. There was a huge PYTHON terrorizing the hens. "Get OUT! Get OUT!" They began to scream.

But the Python looked calmly up . . . and began to SPEAK to them.

"Don't be afraid of me. I won't hurt your chickens. I just came to see your beautiful daughter. I want to marry your daughter. Can I come up and marry your daughter?"

The mother and girl both screamed at once.

"No! NO WAY! Can't marry a SNAKE!"

"Ohhh. Then I will be SO sad. I will have to CRY."

And the Python bent his head and began to weep.

"Boo. Boo-hoo. Boo-hoo-hoo-hoo . . . ."

As he wept, great tears rolled down onto the ground. Soon the ground around his body was covered with a huge puddle. Then he lifted his head and looked at the girl.

"Girl? Look down. See all this? This is how much I love you."

"Now can I come up and marry your daughter?"

But both girl and mother shouted back,

"No! NO WAY! Can't marry a SNAKE!"

"Then I will be SO sad. I will have to CRY some more."

And the snake bent his head and began to cry.

"Boo. Boo-hoo. Boo-hoo-hoo-hoo."

He cried until the house was standing in a small POND of water.

"Girl? Look down. See how much I love you? I REALLY love you!"

"Now can I come up and marry your daughter?"

"NO! NO WAY! Can't marry a SNAKE!"

'Then I will have to cry some more."

And the python bent his head and wept.

"Boo. Boo-hoo. Boo-hoo-hoo-hoo."

Now the water was rising under the house. It was coming right up the pilings.

It was coming up through the floor.

"Girl? Look around. See how much I love you? I REALLY, REALLY love you!"

"Now can I come up and marry your daughter?"

The girl and her mother were scrambling to get up on top of the house, out of the water.

"NO! No WAY! Can't marry a SNAKE!"

"Then I will have to cry some more."

"Boo. Boo-hoo. Boo-hoo-hoo-hoo."

That snake cried until the water rose up through the house. It almost covered the roof. The girl and her mother had only one small spot to stand on to keep their feet dry. They were about to be drowned.

The mother and the daughter looked at each other. "Do you think I should marry him?"

"If you don't, we're *both* going to drown."

"OK! OK! I'll marry you!"

"Then I will be SO happy! I won't cry any more."

Gradually the waters went down. The girl and her mother came down from the roof.

"Now may I come up and visit your daughter?"

"Yes. Come up."

The Python came up the ladder into the house.

"I am SSSSOOOO happy. I am SSSSOOOO happy. I am SSSSOOO happy to be here."

"Now, shall I stay here . . . or would you like to see *my* house."

"Let's go have a look at *his* house," said the mother. "We might as well see what we've gotten ourselves into."

So they followed the snake as he slithered down the river bank . . . farther . . . and farther . . . away from their village . . . farther and farther, and there was a large longhouse!

The snake called up, "Mother! Mother! I have brought home a bride! Can we come up?"

The snake's mother came out and looked down at them.

"Oh my. . . a bride and a mother-in-law too! Yes, yes, there is no sickness or sadness in this house. You can come up."

So the girl and her mother went up into the snake's home. The snake worked hard and put up walls to make a room for them.

When night came the girl and her mother lay down in their own room to sleep. And the snake coiled up by the door.

Early in the morning, before it was even light, the snake awoke. He lifted his head from his coil and looked at the girl.

"Wife . . . .wife . . . have you gone to fetch the water yet?"

She was still sleeping.

So the snake uncoiled his body, stood straight up, peeled off his snakeskin, and he was a handsome young man!

Quickly he climbed down the ladder, took his fishing net from beneath the house, took down the ladle for water, and went to the river. There he threw his nets and caught fish, dipped fresh water, and hurried back home.

He cleaned the fish, made a little fire, boiled rice, and prepared breakfast. He put the rich and fish on a little tray and carried it up to his wife's room.

Then he put back on his snakeskin, coiled up once more, lifted his head and called:

"Wife . . . wake up! Your breakfast is ready!"

The girl awoke and saw her breakfast! "Mother, wake up! The snake has cooked for us!"

She and her mother hurried out to brush their teeth and wash. Then they came back and sat down to a good breakfast.

"This husband is OK! He can really provide for us!"

Next morning the same thing.

Before it was even light, the snake lifted his head and called:

"Wife . . . wife . . . did you go for water yet?"

And when she did not answer, he stood straight up, took off his snakeskin, went to catch fish and fetch water, cooked the breakfast, brought it up, put back on his snakeskin, and called,

"Wife . . . wake up! Your breakfast is ready!"

"This husband is really something! He provides for us so well."

But the girl thought, "I can see how a snake could go to the river and catch fish. But how can a snake cook breakfast?"

So that night the girl stayed awake. All night long she waited and watched.

Just before dawn, when it was still dark, the snake stirred itself. It lifted its head and called,

"Wife . . . did you go for water yet?"

She kept very still.

And she saw the snake . . . .

He stood straight up, peeled off his skin, and was a handsome young man!

Oh! She was so excited! But she did not make a sound. As soon as he had gone down the ladder, that girl grabbed the snakeskin and hid it. Then she went to the top of the ladder and waited. When the snake-man returned she laughed.

"I have CAUGHT you! You are not a snake at all! You are a handsome young man! And you are my husband!"

And he laughed and said,

"That is right! And *you* finally got up before dawn!"

Then he leaped up the ladder and she gave him such a hug.

"Mother!" he called. "Now we can have the wedding celebration!"

So they hung the big gongs for the men to play, and set up the little gongs for the women to play.

And when his relatives arrived they all came up into the house.

They played and they danced and they sang!

They played and they danced and they sang!

All night long!

And in the morning the Python-husband said, "What a PARTY! But I have *friends* who should be here."

So they sent for the Python's friends. And they came up into the house.

They played and they danced and they sang!

They played and they danced and they sang!

All night long!

In the morning the Python-husband said, "What a PARTY! But don't *you* have relatives who should be here?"

So they sent for the girl's relatives.

They played and they danced and they sang!

They played and they danced and they sang!

All night long!

In the morning the husband said, "What a PARTY! But don't you have *friends* who should be here?"

So they sent for the girl's friends.

They played and they danced and they sang!

They played and they danced and they sang!

All night long!

For *seven* days and nights they kept that up!

But on the eighth morning, the wedding guests all said, "What a PARTY! We have to go home now."

And they all climbed down the ladder and got into their canoes and paddled away.

When they had all gone home, the house was so sweetly quiet and empty. The Python-husband and his new bride, and his mother and her mother all settled down to a very happy life in their house beside the river.

**Fruit in Kelantan market,
including imported apples
from the United States!**

Traditional food stand in Kelantan. Coconut juice is available.

**Kelantan museum in
Kota Bahru**

Dinner with Suraya Arrifin and her parents in Batu Gadjah, Perak

Malay woman wearing beautiful,
bright *kebaya*

Malay mother welcoming
visitors to her home in Sabah

Sewn beanbags for playing "five stones"

Children waiting for a snack

Countryside near Malacca

High rises towering over old-style homes in Singapore

Kuching, capital of Sarawak

Traditional Dyak house in Sarawak folk museum

Sabah librarians shared Kadazandusun stories. (For tales told by Yunis Rojin, in the gold dress, see pages 83–95.)

Schoolchildren in Ranau, Sabah

Author with teachers in Ranau, Sabah

School's out at a rural school in the hills above Kota Kinabalu

THE WHITE CROCODILE

From a telling by Abdul Rahman Bulinti Lindas of Kampong Butu Putih, on the Kinabatangan River, Sabah

*T*here once was a young girl who was warned by a fortune teller never to go near the river. It was said that she would be eaten by a crocodile before the age of seventeen. This girl really wanted to swim in the river. She begged and begged her father. But he refused to let her even go near the river. The girl kept pleading with her father to let her go swimming. At last he relented. But her father put guards on the river to make sure no crocodiles came near. Then the girl was allowed to go into the water. How happy she was! She played in the water and swam about; it was so cool and refreshing, this is what she had always longed to do. Every day she would get to swim now. What fun! With the men watching for crocs, it was perfectly safe, she thought.

But far inland on the Sugana River lived a crocodile who heard what the girl was up to. He made his way to the Lukan River, where the girl was swimming. Then this crocodile turned himself into a small lizard, Balinko, and crawled slowly from rock to rock until he reached the water. As soon as he touched the water, he turned back into a crocodile and killed the girl!

The rocks where the lizard crawled down to the water are still there in the Lukan River.

The marauding croc then put the girl's body on his head and went back to his own river. To everybody he passed he called out, "Tell everyone that I have taken the girl and will marry her."

As he passed one human village, a wedding ceremony was going on. It so happened that this girl's own brother was a guest at the wedding. When the brother realized that the crocodile was carrying his sister upstream balanced on his head, the brother was horrified. He knew he had to save his sister. Thinking of a plan, he called to the crocodile, "Can I have a look at your bride? She looks very beautiful, could you bring her closer to the shore so we can see?" And thus he lured the croc closer and closer to the shore, until he was able to grab his sister's body from the croc's head. Wildly, he stabbed the croc with a long stake! "Get away! Get away! Leave my sister alone!"

Now the truth is that if the croc had brought the girl's body home to his own kingdom, he would have been able to revive her and bring her back to life. But now that her brother had snatched the body, the girl remained dead. The brother brought the girl's body back to her village. And the wounded croc swam slowly upstream to his own home.

One day soon after that an old man, Aduk Sabulik Bulik, was bathing by the river when he saw three crocodiles surface. A White Crocodile was in the middle. The White Croc revealed that he was the grandson of the Crocodile King. The Crocodile King was mortally wounded, and they begged Aduk Sabulik Bulik, who knew medicines, to come to the Crocodile Kingdom and heal their king.

The family of Aduk Sabulik Bulik pleaded with him not to go to the Crocodile Kingdom.

"Do not fear," said the White Croc. "We promise that we will not kill you. Only please come and heal our king."

So Aduk Sabulik Bulik's people agreed to let him go. "But he must return in seven days," said the people. "If he does not return, on the eighth day we will poison your river."

Aduk Sabulik Bulik was told then to close his eyes and not open them until told he could do so. The crocs swam with him for some long distance. But he kept his eyes closed the whole way and did not know where they were taking him. At last they said, "You may open your eyes now. We have arrived."

Such a beautiful land! It was just like a human land. There were people all around. The White Crocodile had turned into a prince. And the other two crocs had turned into his body guards. And there, lying on the throne, was the Crocodile King, with a stake in his side. "Here is my Grandfather," said the White Crocodile. "Please, can you heal him?"

Aduk Sabulik Bulik asked for a bamboo, some ashes, and a mosquito net. He warned everyone to leave the room and not to peek at what he was about to do, or they would die. And working his magical healing in secret, Aduk Sabulik Bulik removed the stake from the side of the Crocodile King and placed herbs into the crocodile's body to heal the wound.

The crocodiles were so grateful. "What can we give you?" They offered many wondrous gifts. But Aduk Sabulik Bulik refused them all. "I ask only one thing. In the future do not ever hurt my children, or my children's children, or my children's children, until the end of time. And should you ever break this promise, may my curse be upon you to die."

"And now," said Aduk Sabulik Bulik, "I must return to my village. It is the sixth day already. And I must reach home by the seventh day, or my people will poison your river."

So the crocodiles returned Aduk Sabulik Bulik to his home.

If you go to swim in the Kinabatangan River today, check the bamboos in the water and look around for crocodiles. Speak softly and say that you are relatives of Aduk Sabulik Bulik. And you should be safe to swim.

But just to be sure, never turn your back on the river. And always keep your eye on the crocodiles.

About this story: *This story was told to Margaret Read MacDonald and Jen and Nat Whitman during a homestay evening in Kampong Batu Putih on the Kinabatangan River in Sabah in April 2003. Abdul Rahman Bulinti Lindas told us this story. He and his sister, Mastia Bulinti, had come to the house where we were staying, along with many other people who came to hear their stories. The stories were translated from Sungai into Malay by a villager and then from Malay into English by a Malay-speaking woman visiting from Kota Kiabalu. I scribbled the tale into a notebook as I listened, asking some questions afterward to fill in details. Audience members called out the names of favorite stories and kept a string of tales coming from Abdul and Mastia. They both seemed to know all of the stories and would decide between them who would tell each tale.*

Kampong Batu Butih is part of a government-sponsored homestay program in Sabah. The idea is to provide villages a way to earn income through displaying their traditional lifestyle. This village had a lively teenage dance group and also two respected storytellers. When we arrived the kids were practicing their dances in one of the homes. Since the houses do not have furniture, the living areas are versatile. The dancers could practice easily in the living room of the home. In the evening about thirty people crowded into the same space to hear Abdul and Mastia share stories. Sitting on the floor, many people can enjoy a group event in a small space. The next morning the room was occupied by a teenager lying on the floor staring at the TV in the corner, a grandmother playing with a baby, and three women sewing costumes for the teenage dancers, with still plenty of free space for other activities to take place. The villagers take turns hosting the homestay guests. Thus the income helps the whole village and no one family is overburdened with hosting responsibilities. See the Miso Walai homestay Web site at http://www.borneonativehomestay.com/PeopleSay/index.htm.

THE ORIGIN OF LEECHES

A Sungai tale; told by Abdul Rahman Bulinti Lindas at Kampong Batu Putih

A man and his wife had been married for many years. But still they were without a child. They wanted a child so badly.

One day, when they were out looking for food in the forest, they saw something strange. There was a small child sitting on a tree. There were no people around at all, just this baby all by itself.

"Maybe, maybe this is a gift from the god? Maybe the child was left for us?" The couple brought the baby home.

How happy they were! After a while the baby began to cry.

"Oh! He is hungry!" The woman held the baby tight and it began to suckle. As it sucked at the new mother's breast milk, the baby began to turn bright red. And the baby began to swell up!

"Oh! Something is wrong!" The woman tried to remove the baby from her breast, but it held tight. And the baby kept getting bigger and bigger.

"Husband, help! This cannot be a real baby. It is turning into a monster!"

Sure enough, the baby just kept growing and growing, and it had turned bright red like blood by now. The woman was getting weaker and weaker as the "baby" sucked the life blood out of her.

The man tried to pull the monster child from his wife. But the huge 'baby' would not let go.

Desperate, the husband drew his parang knife and finally just whacked the monster loose. With a huge toss, he threw the creature out of the house.

But the monster rose up, redder than ever. The man ran out and began to whack and whack. Soon the creature was in a million pieces.

The man leaned against a tree, panting. At last the creature was dead. But no, as he watched, each piece of the monster turned into a black leech swollen with blood and began to crawl off into the forest.

There the leeches wait today. And if you come near one, it will fasten onto your skin and begin to suck, and suck, and suck, Only blood will satisfy these creatures.

About this story: Told by Abdul Rahman Bulinti Lindas of Kampong Butu Putih, on the Kinabatangan River, Sabah, April 2003. For more information on the storytelling, see the note after "The White Crocodile" on page 105.

WHY DOG IS TREATED WELL

A Murut tale

*O*nce a Murut man was out hunting when he became lost. He wandered for days and was about to starve from hunger. He found some fruits and berries, but they were not enough. Just when he thought he could not go on longer, he noticed that his dog was digging away at a root. When the dog had dug the root out, it began to gnaw on it.

"If the dog can eat this root, then it should be safe for me to eat, too," thought the man. And he grabbed up a piece and chewed it. Sure enough, it was food.

The next day the man gathered more of this root and filled his basket. Revived now, he managed to find his way home at last.

He showed everyone the root that had saved him from starvation, and they planted the roots he had carried home. In time they grew, and everyone could try them. They were delicious. This was the plant called tapioca. It is used today in many dishes and also fermented to make tapai drink. The tapioca plant is now a staple of the Murut people.

The Murut still remember the dog who discovered this plant, and they treat all dogs very well. It is said that people traveling nowadays on the Kiningau-Tulid road in Sabah are surprised to see Murut people carrying dogs in baskets on their backs, while the small children have to walk. The beloved dog gets a free ride when it gets tired!

Tales from Sarawak

Sarawak is home to many indigenous peoples with amazing folktales. In this section we share tales from Dayak peoples, including Iban and Penan tellers.

THE SQUIRREL AND THE FOREST GECKO

A Penan (Dyak) folktale from Sarawak

*F*orest Gecko and Squirrel went hunting. They had a little hunting hut together, and both went off hunting by themselves during the day.

That evening Squirrel brought home a wild boar.

"What good luck!" Gecko congratulated Squirrel. "You caught a wild boar!"

"This was not *luck*." Replied Squirrel. "I walked a long way and took a lot of trouble to get this wild boar."

"Well, would you give me its skin, so I can barbecue it?" asked Gecko.

"Certainly not. If I give you its skin, what will hold its flesh together?" responded Squirrel.

"Well then, would you give me its feet?"

"Of course not! What would it do without feet?"

So Squirrel kept all of the meat of the wild boar.

Next day Gecko climbed a *laran* tree and shook the branches. All of the bugs and fruit and flowers of the *laran* tree fell into the river below. Many fish came to eat the bugs, fruit, and flowers. Gecko was able to catch a whole basket full of fish.

That night Squirrel congratulated Gecko on his catch. "What a lucky person you are, Gecko! You caught many fish!"

"What do you mean lucky? I had to go far downriver and work hard to catch these fish," replied Gecko.

"Well, would you give me some of the scales to eat?" asked Squirrel.

"Certainly not! What would hold the fish bodies together?" fussed Gecko.

"Well, would you share the fish stomach with me then?"

"How can I give you the fish stomach?" said Gecko. "The fish needs its stomach."

So Forest Gecko and Squirrel each smoked his own catch. And when everything was ready the next day they went home.

Their wives hurried out to greet them. But when the wives looked into the hunting baskets they were confused.

"Why is there only smoked boar meat in one basket and only smoked fish in the other? Didn't the two of you divide between yourselves the meat and the fish?" asked the wives.

"Squirrel wouldn't share with me," grumbled Forest Gecko. "So I wouldn't share with him."

Squirrel's wife took a wooden spoon and BANG! She whopped Squirrel on the head. "What do you mean by not sharing?"

Forest Gecko's wife took a wooden comb and BANG! She whopped Gecko hard on the back. "You know you are supposed to share!"

"I can't believe our husbands could be so stingy," said Squirrel's wife.

"Yes," said Gecko's wife, "every Penan knows that it is the custom to always share food."

Today Squirrel still has a white spot on his head. This is where his wife hit him with a spoon. And Forest Gecko has the mark of a comb on his back. When the Penan people see this, they remember how important it is to always be kind and share your food.

THE LIAR'S PILE

An Iban (Dyak) folktale from Sarawak

*E*veryone knows that lying is wrong. But sometimes children don't realize just how important it is to always tell the truth. Spreading rumors and lies can cause much damage.

One day when a group of young Iban boys were out in the forest, they began to dare each other to climb a tall tree. First one boy tried and then another. At last Tedong's turn came. He was brave and strong. Higher and higher he climbed. Everyone watched in awe, and then the branch he was hanging from broke.

Tedong crashed down and hit the ground hard. The boys clustered around Tedong. He was winded and bruised. But he was not dead, thank goodness. After a while, he recovered and was able to sit up. Slowly the boys helped him limp back home to the village.

But meanwhile one of the boys, Minggi, had run ahead to spread the news. He met Tedong's mother on the path. "Tedong fell out of a tall tree! I think he's dead!" Tedong's mother almost fainted. She staggered home sobbing. Everyone gathered around her. "My son fell out of a tall tree. He was killed."

One man went to beat the wooden drum to call all of the villagers. "A tragedy has occurred. Tedong has fallen from a tall tree and been killed."

Later that day, when the boys arrived back in the village, everyone gasped. Here was Tedong, very much alive. His mother was so relieved. But everyone was sorry she had gone through such a fright.

"Who said this boy was dead?" asked the head man.

"It was Minggi. He met me on the path and said that Tedong had fallen from a tall tree and been killed."

Minggi hung his head. "I was just talking," he muttered. "Tedong *might* have been killed."

"An untruth is an untruth," said the head man. "Come with me. Where did you meet Tedong's mother?"

Minggi led the way back up the path to the spot where he had met Tedong's mother and told her the lie. All of the villagers followed.

"We could have people throw sticks and stones at you for this untruth. That is what you deserve. But instead we will have people throw sticks at the spot where this untruth occurred. Everyone here, take up a stick. Now throw it down in this spot."

The people picked up sticks. They threw them angrily at the spot where Minggi had told such a horrible untruth. Soon a huge pile of sticks stood beside the path.

"Whenever anyone passes this way in the future," said the head man. "They are to throw a stick on the pile. This is to remind us all that telling a lie has serious consequences."

They say that such "Liar's Piles" can be seen in several places in Sarawak. Everyone who passes places a stick on the pile. And thus everyone remembers the importance of telling the truth.

PROTECTING THE FORESTS OF TANJUNG TAMELAN

An Iban (Dyak) tale from Sarawak

A man from the village of Lundu on the Kayan River once climbed Gunung Gading to cut wood. He reached the top of the mountain and began to hack at a huge tree with his axe. It seemed to him that he heard someone crying as he chopped at the tree. So he stopped and listened. But he didn't hear anything. So he continued to chop and chop, until finally the giant tree fell. But as the tree fell he heard the crash of its falling *and* a scream. "What?" He dropped his axe and jumped back. "I must have been imagining this," he thought, and picked up his axe and began to hack at the fallen tree. But every time he hacked at the tree he heard a terrible *groan*. "What is causing this?"

Then suddenly, beyond the tree, he saw three tall spirits rise up. They looked like old men with long white beards. But they were holding their sides and groaning. "Please do not hack at our tree again. We are the spirits of the forest. It pains us so when you destroy our trees."

"Oh, I am so sorry. I didn't know. Please forgive me, sirs."

"I am Datuk Juang," the tallest spirit introduced himself. "And this is Patinggi Metang." The second spirit bowed. Then Datuk Juang raised his voice and shouted, "And this is Temenggong Marang! He is a little hard of hearing." At that Temmenggong Marang bowed, too.

"All of these forests are under our protection," said Datuk Juang. "Please do not cut down these beautiful old trees. It is a shame to destroy them. Leave the forests of Tanjung Tamelan alone."

"I will tell the people in my village," said the young man. "No one from my village will come to your mountain to cut trees again."

"Then we will help your village," responded Datuk Juang. "Cut this felled tree into seven pieces. From each piece carve a fierce-faced human figure. Stand them up facing downstream. These will be your lookouts. If they see pirates or enemies coming upstream to attack you, they will tell us. Then Temmenggong Marang will fire his big gun! The noise will warn you that trouble is coming.

"I don't mind firing my big gun," said Temmenggong Marang. "The loud noise doesn't bother me at all!"

So the man carved seven figures and set them up facing downstream. Then he bid the three spirits farewell and went back to his village.

Everyone agreed that they must respect the three spirits of the forest. So after that no one cut trees near Tanjung Tamelan. The forests there were left in peace.

But one day a loud gun shot was heard in the longhouse at Lundu. "What can that be?"

Then they realized, it was Temmenggong Marang's big gun. "The pirates must be coming upriver! Quick, women and children hide in the forest! Men, get your weapons and get ready to defend our longhouse!"

But the pirates never reached the longhouse. The three spirits decided to have some fun with them. Changing their voices to sound like the pirate chief and his lookout, they began to call back and forth.

"Wrong way! Wrong way! Turn the boat!" shouted Datuk Juang, making his voice sound like that of the pirate lookout.

"No! No!" shouted Patinggi Metang, using a voice like the pirate chief. "Turn THIS way!"

The pirate boat began to turn first one way and then the other in confusion. The pirates put down their paddles and began to argue.

"Strike him! Kill him!" shouted Datuk Juang.

"Hit him! Throw him in the river!" shouted Patinggi Metang.

The terrified men believed each was turning on the other. They began to stab and fight and continued this until only one man was left alive. That man saw the seven figures on the mountaintop and, thinking they were enemies, he struggled up the mountain and began to hack at two of the figures with his sword.

"Not good!" said Datuk Juang. And he pointed his finger at the pirate. At that, the pirate simply fell down dead.

"Good job!" said the three spirits. "These pirates will not bother our friends!"

After a long time the men of Lundu got into their boats and stealthily rowed downriver to see what had happened. They felt sure they would meet the pirate boat coming upstream. But instead they came upon a sight of devastation. Dead bodies floated in the water near Tanjung Tamelan. And the pirate boat drifted empty. "Look at the guardian figures!" shouted one man. There on the mountaintop, it was clear to see that two of the figures had been hacked. And there beside them was a dead pirate. The three spirits were nowhere to be seen. But it was clear who had finished off these pirates.

"Thank you, Datuk Juang!" shouted the men. "Thank you, Patinggi Metang." And then raising their voices VERY loud they all shouted, "Thank you, TEMENGGONG MARANG! We heard your gun!"

"I never mind a little noise!" came an answer from the mountaintop. "I'm a little deaf, you know!"

A few weeks later the people of Lundu brought a feast to thank the three spirits of Tanjung Tamelan. They played their gongs and beat their drums. The women climbed the hill with trays of delightful foods for the three spirits. They left the food there and hurried back down to the riverside. There they spent the day feasting and enjoying themselves. Then in the evening the men went up the hill to bring back the trays. All of the food had disappeared.

"Thank you, Datuk Juang! Thank you, Patinggi Metang. THANK YOU, TEMENGGONG MARANG! We hope you enjoyed your food!"

The guardian figures at Tanjung Tamelan are gone now, fallen and rotted away in the grass. But to this day the people of the area remember. And no one fells a tree at Tanjung Tamelan.

About this story: *Pirates, robbers who arrive by boat to plunder villages, were a serious threat throughout the Malay archipelago. And to this day pirates ply the seas and attack boats they encounter. The story was written by an Iban teacher whose mother told her these stories.*

MANG ALOI VISITS THE MONKEY PEOPLE

A Land Dayak story; told in 1955 by R. Nyadoh, a Land Dayak man from Tapuh, Serian, as a historical account of Kampong Libur near Serian

*M*ang Aloi lived with his mother in a large Land Dyak village. There were many rich people living there, but Mang Aloi and his mother were poor.

They had good crops of padi, but these were always damaged by the forest monkeys. So Mang Aloi made himself a little hut right in the rice fields. He could watch the padi and chase off any long-tailed monkeys who came to steal. For many days this worked fine.

As soon as a monkey would creep into the rice field, Mang Aloi would be after it to chase it back into the forest. His padi was growing nicely and soon would be ready to harvest.

One afternoon it was very hot and Mang Aloi just couldn't stay awake. He nodded and woke. Nodded and woke. And then he fell sound asleep. As soon as the monkeys realized that Mang Aloi was sleeping, hundreds of monkeys came leaping through the rice fields. They surrounded Mang Aloi. And seeing that he was fast asleep, those monkeys lifted him up and carried out of his rice fields. They carried him onto a small tree at the field's edge. And from that tree on to a bigger tree. And from that tree up to a very high tree. And so on, deeper and deeper until they were in the old jungle. And then deeper yet until at last they reached the top of a giant *tapang,* the tallest tree in the forest. And thus they reached the monkey's own village.

The monkey village was a magic place, high out of sight of men. It was just like a human village! And as soon as the monkey's reached home, they changed their form and became like people.

Mang Aloi awakened when he felt himself being carried up into the treetops. But he realized at once what was happening and kept very still. He did not want to alarm the monkeys in any way for fear they might drop him. When the monkeys put him down, he opened his eyes. These monkeys looked just like humans! Mang Aloi sat up and smiled and began to make friends with these monkey-people.

It happened that the mother of the monkey chief was seriously ill. The monkey people were helpless to make her better. They asked Mang Aloi for help.

Although Mang Aloi was not a doctor, he remembered some things that heal, and he agreed to try. He asked them to cook *pangkang* (fatty rice cooked in bamboo sticks) and to prepare fish and eggs and other good foods. Then Mang Aloi sat on a swing and prayed. For a long time he swung and prayed. Then he took *daun chinchung* leaves and applied them to the ill woman's body. Then he sat on the swing and prayed some more. He swung and prayed for the rest of the night. And by morning, the sick woman was feeling better.

The monkey people were so grateful. They gathered many kinds of foodstuffs and goods to give Mang Aloi as a reward. Then, resuming their monkey forms, they picked him up and carried him out of their village. Down from the huge *tapung* tree. Down to the big trees of the old jungle. Down to the middle-sized trees. Down to the small trees at the forest's edge. And back into his own padi fields. There they filled his hut with food and treasures. Now they showed Mang Aloi that they had also brought for him one huge old jar, a *Tajau Ringkung*, full of gold!

Mang Aloi's hut was stuffed with goods! His mother sent villagers to help carry all these goods into the village to her house. There was so much that it took every man in the village to carry it. Mang Aloi himself carried the *Tajau Ringkung* full of gold. Now Mang Aloi was the richest man in the village. So Maung Aloi became head man. To celebrate, he shared his wealth by giving a feast for the village. It lasted for seven days and seven nights!

But in every village there are some who are jealous. Biku was a jealous one. He thought he too should be able to get goods from the forest monkeys. So he went into the fields to sleep as Mang Aloi had done. The very first day he was there he lay down and pretended to be asleep. Sure enough, the monkeys came racing out to examine him. And soon they were carrying him off. First onto the small tree, then to a big tree, eventually into the old jungle, and finally up into the great *tapang* tree. As he felt himself being carried higher and higher, Biku became frightened and could not pretend to be asleep any longer. "Don't drop me! Don't drop me!" he shouted. The startled monkeys shrieked and let go.

Of course he fell. Who knows how far? He was never seen again. So the story of Biku ends right there.

But the story of Mang Aloi continues to this day. The *Tajau Ringkung* is still kept in the village of Ramun, where Mang Aloi's great-great-great-great-great-grandson keeps it hidden in the old jungle. And each year at harvest time, Mang Aloi's descendants give a feast for the village, just as Mang Aloi did.

The descendants of Mang Aloi are:

> Mang Aloi
> Miyai
> Badang
> Julai
> Mariben
> Rapak
> Dingun Lidang

In 1955, when this story was told, Dingun Lidang was head chief at Kampong Libur near Serian. The jar was kept by his father, Rapak.

Tales from Brunei

Lying between Sarawak and Sabah, the country of Brunei is home to some of the same ethnic groups. Thus the story here is from the Dusun people, who also live in Sabah.

THE DOLLARBIRD AND THE SHORT-TAILED MONKEY

A Dusun folktale from Brunei

*S*hort-Tailed Monkey came to spend the night in the tall tree where Dollarbird perched.

"Don't stop here!" called Dollarbird. "You can't sleep in my tree. I have a very loud voice. I will be calling to the Lord early in the morning. Go sleep somewhere else."

"I can sleep here if I want to," replied Short-tailed Monkey. And the monkey made her nest right there under the Dollarbird's nest.

"I am warning you again," called down the Dollarbird. "I cry out to the Lord during the night. And I have a very loud voice. You do not want to sleep near me."

But the monkey ignored this warning and moved in with her baby monkey and settled down for the night beneath the perch of the Dollarbird.

Sure enough, in the dark of the night, before dawn had arrived, a loud "Langou! Langou!" sounded from the top of the tree. The Dollarbird was calling out to the Lord. The bird's call was so strong that the baby monkey was startled and fell right out of the nest.

The Short-tailed Monkey was furious. She grabbed the Dollarbird by its wings and proceeded to pluck out all of its feathers! The poor bird fell to the ground shivering and tried to cover itself with leaves. Unable to fly, the bird appealed to the Lord day and night. "Langou! Langou!" For one day, two days, three days, the Dollarbird called out to the Lord. And the bird's feathers grew back. It could fly again.

But the Dollarbird was not satisfied. Now it began to petition the Lord to make all the trees die to punish the Short-tailed Monkey and her people. Day and night the Dollarbird called out to the Lord. "Langou! Langou!" The bird never ceased in its loud calling. And sure enough, the Lord granted the bird's request. Now all of the trees in the area died.

When the trees were dead, the grass, the drinking water, everything began to die. And soon there was nothing for the animals to eat. So the animals began to die, too. At last only two of each species was left. There were two Long-tailed Monkeys, two Short-tailed

Monkeys. Two Wild Boars, two Mouse Deer, two Santhur Deer, and two Barking Deer. Just a male and female of each species . . . that was all that survived.

The animals met to discuss this situation. They decided they must call the Dollarbird to return from across the water, where it had flown. They must get it to come back and petition the Lord for relief.

But who could make the long journey across the sea to reach the Dollarbird?

"Not us," said the Lesser Squirrels and the Greater Squirrels. "We can climb the dead trees and eat the bark. That's all we need. We aren't going to risk that just to get food." So they scrambled up into the trees and refused to help.

"I will try," said Gecko. And Gecko started out for the sea. When he reached the beach he could not see land, even far away. So he stuck out his long tongue to see what he could reach. He stuck it out, and stuck it out, until "Aack!" with a cracking sound Gecko's jaw locked! "Too far," Gecko muttered as he returned. "Too far for me." But his tongue is still very long.

White-bodied Wood Beetle tried next. It flew aloft through seven layers of clouds. But still it could not see even a shadow of land. Then it fell whirring into the sea and was almost swallowed by a fish! "Burrr . . . burrr." The beetle hurried back home. "I flew as far as I could. I didn't see even the shadow of a land." The Wood Beetle by this time had been blackened by the sun. And so it remains to this day.

"Is anyone strong enough to go?" asked the animals once more.

"I will try," said Tiger Butterfly. "If I get there I will let you know. And even if I don't, I'll tell you, too." And Tiger Butterfly flew off. On and on flew Tiger Butterfly until it could go no more. So it settled down on some sea foam to rest. Until a fish lunged for it! Then up it flew, and on and on, resting on the sea foam when it needed. Flying away when danger approached, on and on, until at last it could see just the shadow of the tip of an island ahead. "I think I can make it. I just have to keep going, " At last the exhausted butterfly reached the island. There were trees hanging heavy with fruit. So heavy that the branches nearly touched the ground.

After reviving for a moment, Tiger Butterfly went in search of the Dollarbird. "You must come back and call to the Lord to help us now," pleaded Tiger Butterfly. "Everything has died where we live. And of all the animals, only two of each kind remain. Please come back and remove your curse."

"Yes," replied the Dollarbird. "I feel pity for you now. If it is as you say and all of your food is gone and animals are dying, I will return and ask the Lord to help you."

Relieved, the Tiger Butterfly began its journey back across the sea. But many days before the butterfly reached home, the fast-flying Dollarbird had already arrived. And once again the Dollarbird's prayer echoed throughout the forest. "Langou! Langou!" And within a week these calls had brought back life. The trees were budding once more, shoots of grasses and plants were sprouting from the earth. And the animals had food again at last.

However the Dollarbird did not remain in the land. Having done its work to bring back fruit to the land, the Dollarbird flew away. Each August it returns though, just in time to enjoy the fruiting of the trees.

About this story: *The Dollarbird is a broad-billed roller* (Eurystomus orientalis). *It has silver-dollar-sized spots on its wings. This bird returns to Borneo every year just after the rainy season, when the trees blossom and bear fruit. Versions of this story are told by the Iban and Penan people of Sarawak as well as by the Dusun, who told this version. Sometimes the bird is said to have flown all the way to Sumatera, a large Indonesian island quite a distance from Borneo.*

THE KING OF THE MOSQUITOES

A folktale from Brunei Darussalam

*T*here once were two sisters. Aminah, the elder, was rather grumpy and not a very kind person. Her younger sister, Rokiah, seemed always to think of helping others and showed kindness at all times.

One day the sisters were sent by their mother to gather nipa palms to repair their house's roof. Unfortunately the place where the nipa palms grew was home to many, many mosquitoes. The tiny insects lit all over their bodies. Aminah slapped at them and killed as many as possible. But Rokiah simply waved her hands and tried to shoo them away without harming the little creatures.

When the mosquitoes continued flocking around her, Rokiah spoke to them. "Dear mosquitoes, won't you take me to your King? I would ask him to allow us to work in peace here."

"You want to meet our king? Aren't you afraid?" buzzed the mosquitoes.

"I am not afraid of any creature. I am sure your King is capable of kindness."

So the mosquitoes gathered around Rokiah and flew with her to the place where their King was waiting.

But when she saw the King of the Mosquitoes, Rokiah did almost die of fright. His eyes were as big as limes, he teeth were as big as bananas, his antennae were long and curling down to his stomach. The King of the Mosquitoes was so huge and frightening to look on that Rokiah fainted.

When she awoke, she was lying in a hut, and bending over her was the frightful King of the Mosquitoes. But she didn't want to show her fear. She didn't want to let the creature know that she found him repulsive.

"My dear girl, it is time to eat," said the King of the Mosquitoes. "There is rice, water, a cooking pot, and firewood here. Go ahead and prepare food."

Rokiah looked where he pointed. The "rice" was really a bag of worms. The "water" was really blood. And the cooking pot was an old skull. Rokiah felt horror when she looked

---

at these things. But she did not want to show ingratitude to the King of the Mosquitoes. So she politely prepared the food.

When the King of the Mosquitoes had eaten, he nodded to Rokiah. "Now what can I do for you?"

"I think I have stayed here too long, kind King. May I go home now?"

"Of course, my child. But let me send a gift with you." And the King of the Mosquitoes brought out a small black box.

"When you reach home you may open the box," said the King of the Mosquitoes. "But before you open it, you must prepare things properly. You must put up seven layers of *lawangan* nets and fasten them down tightly with stones."

Rokiah thanked the King of the Mosquitoes, and hurried home with the black box.

She told her mother all about her adventure in the land of the mosquitoes and showed her the little black box. "But we must set up many *lawangan* nets before we open it," she told her mother. "And fasten them down well with stones."

Their family had only one net, but they borrowed nets from the neighbors and soon had arranged things just as the King of the Mosquitoes had advised. Then gently Rokiah lifted the lid of the black box. Sparkles began to shoot from the box in all directions. They hit the nets and stuck there or fell back onto the ground. Soon the area was covered with gold and diamonds!

When Aminah saw all this, she was so jealous of her little sister. "You got all of this from the King of the Mosquitoes? I will go and get a box for myself!"

"But I will share my gold and diamonds with you," offered Rokiah. But Aminah wanted a hoard of treasure all for herself. She rushed off to the nipa palm grove.

As soon as the mosquitoes began to buzz about, Aminah trapped one in her hands. "Take me to your King!" she demanded. "I have come to get treasure like my sister has!"

The poor little insect buzzed the word, and many mosquitoes flew in to carry Aminah to the King of the Mosquitoes.

When Aminah encountered the King of the Mosquitoes, she was so horrified that she too fainted. But when she awoke and found the King of the Mosquitoes bending over her, she had no desire to hide her disgust. "YUCK! Get away from me!" she cried.

The King of the Mosquitoes felt wounded by her words, but he kindly offered to have her prepare food, just as he had done with Rokiah. When Aminah saw the "rice" worms, the "water" blood, and the "pot" skull, she could not hide her revulsion. "Disgusting! No way will I touch this gross stuff! Just give me my gift and I will go home."

"Well, we do have a gift for you, girl." And the King of the Mosquitoes brought out a large black box. "But be sure to set up nets before you open it . . . ."

Aminah was already rushing off home, hauling the big black box back. Her mother had prepared a space within nets for her to open the box. Aminah rushed into the enclosure and ripped off the lid. AAACK! From the box slithered dozens of poisonous snakes!

Such is the reward for unkindness in folktales, and such is the reward for kindness, too.

DAYANG BONGSU AND THE CROCODILE

A Dusun tale from Brunei

*L*ittle Dayang Bongsu was captured by a crocodile! The giant croc swam with her to an island in the middle of the river and left her there. "Just wait here, my sweet," said the croc. "I will prepare a house for you at my home under the water." And the crocodile disappeared under the brown, murky waters of the river.

Poor little Dayan Bongsu cried and cried. "Oh no! Oh no! The croc will eat me!"

UP popped the croc. "What was that, my sweet?"

"Oh, I was just saying "So hot. So hot. It is so hot up here."

"Don't worry, my sweet. I have already started your house. I am putting in the house posts just now." And the croc dove under the water again.

"Oh no! Oh no! The croc will eat me!"

UP came the croc again. "What's that, my sweet?"

"Oh, it is just so hot. So hot. It is so hot up here."

"I am working swiftly, my sweet. Already the floor joists are being put in place for your house." And the croc disappeared under the water.

Just then Dyang Bongsu saw a santhur-deer passing by. "Oh please, dear Santhur-Deer, come and rescue me!"

"Hold onto my tail then," said the santhur-deer. "I will swim to the shore." But when the small deer started to swim, the girl's weight pulled it under.

"Let go! Let go! You can drown if you like. But I don't want to die too!" And the santhur-deer swam away.

The girl began to wail again. "Oh no! Oh no! The croc will eat me!"

UP rose the croc! "What's that, my sweet?"

"Oh, it is so hot here. So hot."

"Never mind, my sweet. Already I am putting up the walls. I will bring you below the water soon." And the croc plunged back into the river.

But here came a wild boar. "Wild boar! Wild boar! Please, pull me to the shore!"

"Very well. Hold onto my tail. I will swim to the shore," agreed the wild boar.

But as soon as he started swimming, her weight pulled him under.

"No! No! Let go! You can drown if you like. But I do not want to die too!"

Now the girl was crying harder than ever. "Oh no! Oh no! The croc will eat me!"

UP popped the croc! "What's that, my sweet?"

"Oh, it is so hot. So very hot."

"Soon you will be cool, my sweet. Already I am putting on the roof rafters." And the croc dove once more.

Just then a mouse deer came by. "Please! Please Mouse Deer! Rescue me!"

"Well, hold onto my tail," said Mouse Deer. " I will drag you to shore." But no sooner had she grabbed onto his tail than he began to sink under the water.

"Let go! Let go! You can drown if you like. But I do not want to die too!"

"Oh no! Oh no! The croc will eat me!"

UP came the croc! "What's that, my sweet?"

"Oh, I was just crying because it is so hot. So hot here."

"I am just putting on the roof, my sweet. Soon I will come for you." And the croc slipped into the dark water once more.

Now a long-tailed monkey came by. "Oh, Monkey, PLEASE, PLEASE save me!"

"Well, hold onto the tip of my tail," said the monkey. "I believe I can tow you to the shore."

"Wait," said Dayang Bongsu. "I am going to leave a little flea behind."

To the flea, she said, "Please, friend flea, if the crocodile calls, answer him and pretend it is my voice."

"No problem," said the flea. "I will do just that."

So holding tight to the very tip of the long-tailed monkey's tail, Dayang Bongsu was towed slowly to the shore.

Meanwhile the croc had emerged and called to her, "Are you about ready to come to your new home, Dayang Bongsu?"

"Oh yes," answered the flea, in a voice like that of Dayang Bongsu. "But I am preparing my appearance. Just wait a few moments."

The croc dove down and worked more on the house, then arose again.

"Are you ready now, Dayang Bongsu?"

"Oh yes," answered the flea. "But I need a bit more time to arrange my hair."

And so it went, until Dayang Bongsu and the long-tailed monkey were safely ashore and had escaped into the forest.

How sad the croc was when he realized that Dayang Bongsu had escaped. But how happy she was to be on dry land at last, safe and sound!

SI PERAWAI, THE GREEDY FISHERMAN

From Brunei Darussalam

*I*t is said that there once lived a fisherman named Si Perawai. No matter how much Si Perawai had, he always wanted more. And one day he got "more." But sometimes "more" can be "too much."

It was just an ordinary day to begin with. Si Perawai would throw out his long fishing line, then pull it in. Throw out his long line, then pull it in. All day he had been working like this. But each time he pulled in the line, there was not one fish on the line.

It was getting late in the afternoon, when suddenly he saw all of the floats on his line start to jiggle. Something was on the line! Quickly he started to haul in his catch, whatever it was. But when he pulled the line in, he found that caught on the end of his line was a long chain. At first he thought to toss it back overboard, but then as he looked at it closer he saw a gleam from beneath the sea scum. He rubbed at the chain. OH MY! The chain was solid gold!

Si Perawai held tight to the chain. Its end was still dragging in the water. Perhaps it was longer. Who knew how long?

Si Perawai began to pull the chain's length into the boat. "I can sell this gold chain!" thought Si Perawai. "I will be able to buy a new net, and new fishing lines!"

Then as he realized that the chain was longer than he had at first thought, his dreams began to grow. "This is a LONG golden chain! I will be able to buy a new boat!"

Still the chain did not end. Si Perawai was ecstatic. "I will be able to build a new house!" He exclaimed as he hauled in more and more of the golden chain.

But a little bird began to circle his head. "Cut and go! Cut and go!" called the bird.

The heavy chain was piling up in the boat, coiling round and round, heavier and heavier.

Si Perawai batted the troublesome bird away with his hand. "I will be able to buy more land! I will have new clothing!"

The boat was sinking lower and lower in the water.

"Cut and go! Cut and go!" called the bird, buzzing round and round the head of the crazed Si Perawai.

But Si Perawai had no ears for advice. "I will throw a feast! I will be famous!" Hand over hand, he hauled in more and more of the heavy golden chain. Now the boat had sunk completely into the water, and the water was ready to pour into his boat.

"Cut and go! Cut and go!" screeched the bird.

But now it was too late. With a great swoosh, the boat sank beneath the waves with Si Perawai and the yards and yards of golden chain.

They say the boat full of golden chain still lies beneath the water. But it was never found. All that remains is the tale, a warning to all that it is important to know when to "cut and go!"

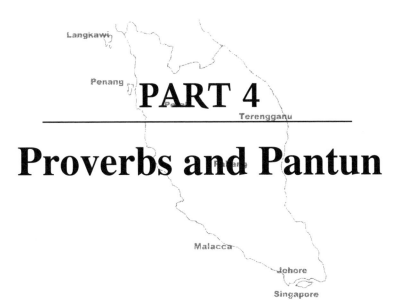

PART 4

Proverbs and Pantun

*T*his section shares proverbs and the Malay poetic form called *pantun*. You can learn a lot about a culture from its proverbs. What can you learn about the Dusun and Malay peoples from these proverbs? Do the proverbs seem true to you? Do you have similar proverbs in your own culture?

DUSUN PROVERBS

The Dusun people live on the island of Borneo. These Dusun proverbs are from Kahung Sariyoh on the Tempasuk (Kedamaian) River.

Magadau montaun-taun, songadau noh rumasam aiopos naik.

Though there is fine weather year after year, a day's rain will wet everything.

This is said of a man who has a good reputation, but ruins it all with one bad action.

Sanginan do karaboh minongoiit do borutak nopihidan ngail 'o tulan do sompomogunan.

A single buffalo brought mud, and all the people of the village are smeared.

Just one person did something wrong, but everyone in the village got a bad name.

Iyoh gontulak nokaolan do tapu.

Like a gecko who has eaten lime.

The gecko's poop is partly white, as if it had eaten white lime. The gecko walks across the ceiling and drops poop on the people below and doesn't even care. It just walks on and does the same thing again. So this saying refers to someone who does a shameful thing and doesn't even care, just goes ahead and does it again.

MALAY PROVERBS

Ayer yang penoh di-dalam tong tiada berkcochak,
Melainkan sa-tengah tong itu.
A bucket full of water does not splash around,
Only a half-full bucket splashes.
In other words, the truly learned are quiet and modest.

Buah padi, makin berisi, makin rendah;
Buah padi yang hampa, makin lama, makin tinggi.
The fuller the ear is of rice grain, the lower it bends,
Empty of grain, it grows taller and taller.
The wise are modest. The empty-headed are assertive.

Kita baharu chapai pengayoh,
Orang sudah tiba ka-saberang.
We have just grabbed our paddles,
They have already crossed the river.

Sa-ēkor kuman dibenua China dapat di-lihat,
Gajah sa-ekor bertenggek di-batang hidong, tiada sedar.
He can see a louse as far away as China,
but is unaware of an elephant on his own nose.

Ladang orang berlari-lari,

Lading sendiri berjangkah-jangkah.

Over the fields of others he goes running,

Over his own he picks his way.

He tramples other people's things, but is careful of his own.

Sa-ekor kerbau membawa lumpor,

semua terpalit.

One muddy buffalo,

the whole herd gets dirty.

Jong pechah, yu sarat.

When a ship breaks up, sharks get their fill.

Ketam menyurohkan anak-nya berjalan betul.

The crab instructed its young to walk straight.

There is a little folktale about this. The mother crab tells her children to walk straight. But then she shows them how by walking sideways, the only way a crab can move.

Kalau telan, mati emak,

Kalau ludah, mati bapa.

Swallow it, one's mother dies,

Reject it, and one's father dies.

This comes from a folktale in which the hero was given two choices: If he took one path his mother would die; if he took the other path he would lose his father. It is said when there is no good choice.

Maskok kawan gajah, mendering.

Masok kawan ayam, berkokok.

Masok kawan kambing, berdebek.

When in a herd of elephants, trumpet.

When in a flock of chickens, crow.

When in a group of goats, bleat.

Queries: Look at the Malay words on page 135. An elephant is *gajah*. A chicken is *ayam*. A goat is *kambing*. Can you tell what Malay word means "trumpet like an elephant"? What is the Malay word for "crow"? What is the Malay word for "bleat"?

Of someone who tries to act as if they are higher than they are, it can be said:

Kachang lupakan kulit.	A bean forgets about its pod.
Anak kuching menjadi harimau.	A kitten has become a tiger.
Belalang telah menjadi lang.	A grasshopper has become a hawk.
Pachat hendak menjadi ular sawa.	A leech wants to become a snake.
Chaching menjadi ular naga.	A worm has become a dragon.
Pipit hendak meminang anak enggang.	A sparrow wants to be engaged to a hornbill.

Pipit itu sama pipit juga,

dan yang enggang sama enggang.

Sparrows must mate with sparrows,

and hornbills with hornbills.

Queries: What do you think the Malay word for "sparrow" is? What is the Malay word for "hornbill"?

Hilang jasa beliong,

timbul jasa rimbas.

The word of the adze is forgotten,

That of the plane gets noticed.

The adze cuts the board and does the hard work. The plane just smoothes the board down at the end. But this is what gets the praise.

Banyak udang, banyak garam-nya.

Banyak orang, banyak ragam-nya.

Many shrimps, many spices.

Many men, many temperaments.

MALAY PANTUN

This form of poetry dates back at least to the fifteenth century. It appeared within the *Sedjaret Malayou* and other early Malay texts. The poetic form has four lines. The first and third rhyme and the second and fourth rhyme. Often the first two lines set up an image and the last two develop that idea. For example:

> *Kerengga dei-dalam buloh*
> *Serahi běrisi ayer mawar*
> *Sampai hasrat di-dalam tuboh*
> *Tuan sa-orang jadi pěnawar.*

> Large ants in the bamboo-cane,
> A flask filled with rosewater.
> When the passion of love seizes me
> From you alone I can expect the cure.

Pantun are used especially in courting. A boy may call one to the girl, and if she is clever, she may reply with an even better pantun. Try reading the Malay out loud. You can hear the fun rhythm and rhyme, even if you don't understand the exact meaning of the words.

Here is one asking a girl to be kind even though the suitor might be poor.

> *Jangan chupar chěmpědak bongkok*
> *Chěmpědak bongkok banyak biji-nya.*
> *Jangan chupar orang burok*
> *Orang muda baik budi-nya.*

> Don't curse the bent jack-fruit
> Even a bent one has many fruits.
> Don't curse a shabby fellow.
> He may well be young and gentle.

Here is one from a youth enamored of a Tamil girl.

Kĕlip-kĕlip api di-dusun;
Anak Keling bĕrgĕlang kacha.
Bukan mati kĕrana rachun,
Mati di-jĕling ekor mata.

In the orchard fireflies flicker;
There's a Tamil girl with fragile bangles.
It's not from poison that I'm dying,
But from her dark sidelong glances.

Here is a pantun to a girl who won't give the young man the time of day.

Bĕrjalan mĕmaroh-maroh,
Dapat limau si-tiga iris.
Bĕrapa-lah rindu abang taroh,
Ayer di-gĕnggam tidak tiris.

Walking ravenous with hunger,
I get what? Three lemon slices.
However much I pine,
Not one drop escapes your fist.

And here is a pantun addressed to a Malaccan girl. She had probably sassed him with a witty pantun, and this is his reply.

Orang haji mĕmasang lukah.
Pasang di-bĕting ikan ta'kĕna.
Sunggoh kĕchil chili Mĕlaka,
Pĕdeh-nya sampai chuping tĕlinga.

The haji sets his fish trap.
Set on the bank, but no fish comes.
In truth it's small, the Malacca chili,
But so hot that even my ears tingle.

Many traditional Malay pantun are remembered and used. But folks also like to make up their own, and the cleverer the better. You might like to try creating a pantun of your own.

Pantun can also be used to create riddles. But this is even more difficult!

Lĕmah lĕmbut tulus mĕsĕra,
Hairan! Takut bukan-nya suatu.
Di-hambat lari bĕrchĕmpĕra,
Tĕtapi bukan-nya shaitan dan hantu.

Gentle, honest and straightforward,
Amazing! Not a few are afraid of him.
He chases them off helter-skelter,
And yet he's no devil or ghost.

Answer: Rain

Ada a-ekor burong dewata,
Kaki-nya panjang bagai sĕnjata.
Kalau dudok tĕmpat yang rata,
Boleh ia bĕrkata-kata.

There is a bird of paradise,
His leg is long like a weapon.
If he sits in a place that is flat,
Then he can talk and talk.

Answer: A pen.

And here is one that only someone who knows Malay food could guess.

Bĕras ladang sulong tahun,
Malam-malam masak nasi.
Dalam batang ada daun,
Dalam daun ada isi.

Grain from the clearing, the year's first fruits,
Every night we cook the rice.
Inside the stem there is a leaf,
Within the leaf is something.

Answer: *Kueh lemang.* This is a yummy food made by stuffing a bamboo tube with sticky rice soaked in coconut milk, wrapped in a banana leaf. The entire thing is braised over a fire, then the banana leaf wrapped sticky rice is removed, the banana leaf packet is opened, and the rice is eaten. YUM!

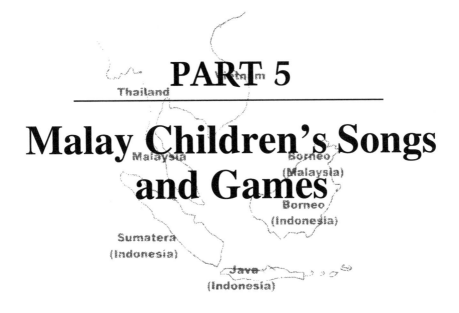

PART 5

Malay Children's Songs and Games

*I*n this section are some favorite songs of Malay children. The song "Bangau o Bangau" is popular throughout Malaysia. Its tune and words vary slightly from place to place, but the sequence of events is similar. "Enjit Enjit Semut" is such a fun action song that even teens love performing it! A Web site is listed below at which you can see Malay teens singing. This section also includes some games popular among Malay children. Another Malay game, top throwing, plays an important part in the story "The Singing Top" (in Part 2).

MALAY CHILDREN'S SONGS

Bangau o Bangau/Egret o Egret

This is one of the most popular children's songs in Malaysia. It was sung to me by librarians in Sabah, Singapore, and Kuala Lumpur. I give the Sabah version here. The Sabah librarians repeat the Egret's answer "Fish does not come up" twice when they sing. Most others I have heard do not repeat the line.

Egret, oh Egret,
Why are you so thin?

How could I not be thin.
Fish does not come up.
Fish does not come up.

Fish, oh Fish,
Why do you not come up?

How could I come up?
Grass is too tall.
Grass is too tall.

Grass, oh Grass,
Why are you so tall?

How could I not be tall?
Kerbau won't eat me.
Kerbau won't eat me.

Bangau o Bangau,
kenapa engkau kurus?

Macam mana aku tak kurus.
Ikan tidak timbul.
Ikan tidak timbul.

Ikan o Ikan,
Kenapa tidak timbul?

Macam mana aku nat timbul?
Rumput panjang sangat.
Rumput panjang sangat.

Rumput o rumput,
Kenapa engkau panjang?

Macam mana aku tak panjang?
Kerbau tak makan aku.
Kerbau tak makan aku.

Kerbau, oh Kerbau,	*Kerbau o Kerbau,*
Why don't you eat grass?	*Kenapa tak makan rumput?*
How could I eat grass?	*Macam mana aku tak makan?*
I have a stomach ache.	*Perut aku sakit.*
I have a stomach ache.	*Perut aku sakit.*
Stomach, oh stomach,	*Perut o perut,*
Why are you in pain?	*Kenapa engkau sakit?*
How could I not be in pain?	*Macam mana aku tak sakit?*
I ate uncooked rice.	*Macan nasih mentah.*
I ate uncooked rice.	*Macan nasih mentah.*
Rice, oh Rice,	*Nasi o nasi,*
Why are you not cooked?	*Kerapa engkau mentah?*
How could I be cooked?	*Macam mana aku tak mentah*
The firewood is wet.	*Kayu api basah?*
The firewood is wet.	*Kayu api basah?*
Wood, oh Wood,	*Kayu o kayu,*
Why are you so wet?	*Kenapa engkau basah?*
How can I not be wet?	*Macam mana aku tak basah?*
Rain falls on me.	*Hujan timpa aku.?*
Rain falls on me.	*Hujan timpa aku.?*
Rain, oh Rain,	*Hujan o hujan,*
Why do you fall on wood?	*Kenapa timpa kayu?*
How could I not fall?	*Macam mana aku tak timpa?*
Frogs are calling me.	*Katak panggil saya.*
Frogs are calling me.	*Katak panggil saya.*

Frog, oh Frog,	*Katak o katak*
Why do you call Rain?	*Kenapa panggil hujan?*
How could I not call Rain?	*Macam mana aku tak panggil?*
Snake wants to eat me.	*Ular nak makan aku.*
Snake wants to eat me.	*Ular nak makan aku.*
Snake, oh Snake,	*Ular o ular,*
Why do you eat Frog?	*Kenapa makan katak?*
How could I not eat frog?	*Macam mana aku tak makan?*
Frog is my FOOD!	*Memang makanan aku!*

(Jump at a child on the word "FOOD.")

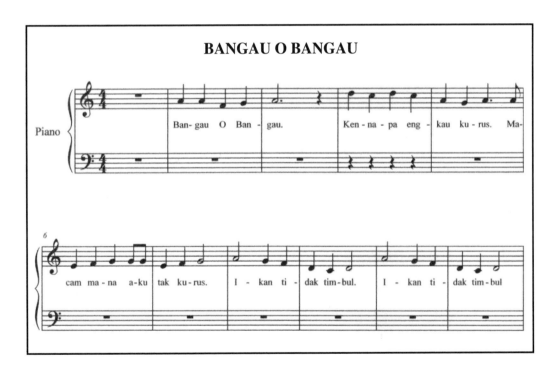

BANGAU O BANGAU

Note: Because this is a folk song, there are many variants. I have provided the tune as it was sung to me by Doretty Sikuat in Kota Kinabalu, Sabah. Doretty and her librarian friends also wrote out the English translation for me. There was much glee at the jumping on the last word of the song.

Burung Kakak Tua/Old Sister Cockatoo

Burung Kakak Tua
Hinggap di jendela
Nenek sudah tua
Giginya tinggal dua.

Lechum, lechum, lechum. hu la la.
Lechum, lechum, lechum. hu la la.
Lechum, lechum, lechum. hu la la.
Burung kaka tua.

Old Sister Cockatoo
Lands on my window.
Granny's getting grey,
Her teeth left only two!

Lechum, lechum, lechum. hu la la.
Lechum, lechum, lechum. hu la la.
Lechum, lechum, lechum. hu la la.
Old Sister Cockatoo!

Burung Kakak Tua

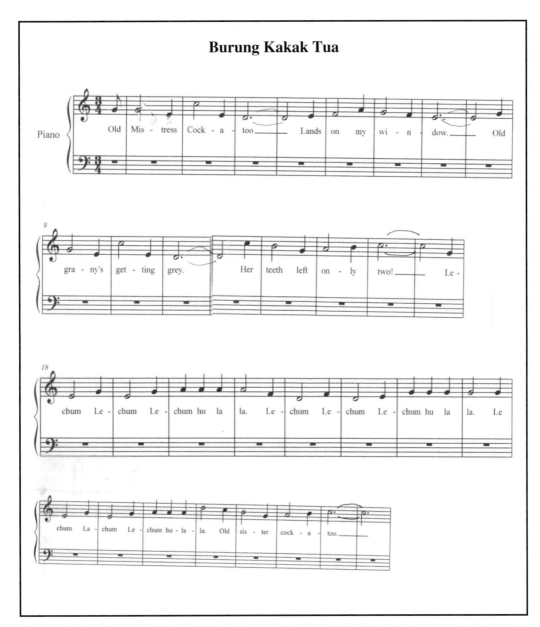

Note: This is a favorite Malay children's song. *Burung Kakak Tua* is the name for the cockatoo, called "Old Sister Bird." You can hear the tune for this song and more commentary at http://www.mamalisa.com/?lang=Malay&t=es&p+856.

Enjit Enjit Semut/Step, Step Ant

This is a singing hand game.

Enjit Enjit Semut
Siapa sakit naik atas.
Enjit Ejit semut
Siapa sakit naik atas.

Step, step ant,
If you are hurt, climb up.
Step, step ant,
If you are hurt, climb up.

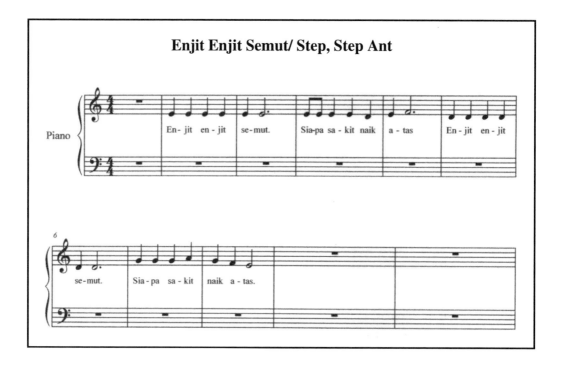

To play this game, players hold out their hands, palm down. Each person lightly pinches the skin on the back of the hand of another player, stacking up their hands in the center of the circle. At the end of each line, the hand on the bottom is lifted above the pile and drops down on the top hand to pinch the top of that hand (gently; this is a little ant stepping on the hand, and at the end of each refrain the bottom ant "climbs up") . Three or four players usually play together at one time. A group of Malay teens performing this song can be seen at http://www.youtube.com/watch?v=NZZHCpZTHpU&mode=related&search=.

At the time of writing this book, there were several YouTube renditions of this song available. Just Google "Enjit Enjit Semut." Teens have fun creating verses to sing between choruses of "Enjit Enjit Semut." A lively "Oi! Oi!" accompanies each verse. For an English-language example, see http://www.youtube.com/watch?v=XhQmBrlyB9M&mode=related&search=.

MALAY CHILDREN'S GAMES

Batu Selimbat: Five Stones

Malay children like to play a game similar to our jacks. It is called "batu selimbat," or "five stones." Originally the game was played with five small stones. But nowadays it is often played with five small triangular shaped bean bags. These can be made from scraps of cloth and stuffed with rice or small beans.

The rules for the game are:

Round one:
1. A player throws the five stones on the ground. One is chosen to toss in the air.
2. The player tosses this stone into the air and must pick up another stone in the same hand and catch the stone tossed into the air, all in one move.
3. The player repeats this, throwing up one stone, but must also pick up a third stone. Now the player has three stones in one hand.
4. The player repeats this, picking up a fourth stone.
5. The player repeats, picking up the fifth stone. Now the player has five stones in one hand!

Round two:
1. The player throws the five stones on the ground, attempting to keep them as close together as possible.
2. The opponent selects one of the stones, usually the one farthest away from the others. This is the one the player must use as a tossing stone.
3. The player puts a thumb and forefinger on the ground, forming an arch. Then the player throws the selected stone into the air, pushes one of the remaining stones through the arch, and catches the falling stone before it hits the ground.

---

4. The player repeats this for each of the other stones.

5. Once all four stones have been pushed through the arch, the player throws the fifth stone in the air one more time, picks up all four stones, and catches the falling stone, all with one hand.

Players take turns attempting the two rounds. If a player fails to catch the stone before it hits the ground, it is another player's turn. The first player to complete the whole sequence without a miss is the winner.

Hantam Bola/Hit Ball

This is a popular Singapore children's game, similar to dodge ball. To play this game you need a soft ball, so as not to injure players.

Rules:
1. Players take turns rolling a ball into a marked goal area about three meters away.

2. Once a player gets a ball into the goal, everyone can rush to grab the ball.

3. The first person to grab the ball tries to throw it and hit someone else.

4. If the person is hit, in other words *hantamed,* the game begins again.

5. If the person is missed, someone else grabs the ball and tries to hit someone with it. This continues until someone is hit.

APPENDIX A:
NOTES ON TALE SOURCES
AND MOTIFS

Sources Consulted

In the notes I give references to folktale motif indexes that have included these stories. The sources I refer to are:

Aarne, Antti, and Stith Thompson. *The Types of the Folktale.* Helsinki: Folklore Fellows Communication, 1961.

MacDonald, Margaret Read. *The Storyteller's Sourcebook: A Subject, Title, and Motif-Index to Folklore Collections for Children.* 1st ed. Detroit: Neal-Schuman/Gale Research, 1982.

MacDonald, Margaret Read, and Brian W. Sturm. *The Storyteller's Sourcebook: A Subject, Title, and Motif-Index to Folklore Collections for Children: 1983–1999.* Farmington Hills, MI: Gale Group, 2000.

Thompson, Stith. *Motif-Index of Folk-Literature.* 6 vols. Bloomington: Indiana University Press, 1966.

You may consult those indexes as well as the sources cited in the tale notes to find more variants of the stories shared here. All tales are retold by Margaret Read MacDonald unless otherwise stated.

Part 2: Tales of the Malay People

Legends of Malacca, Johore, and Singapore from the *Sedjaret Malayou*

A Ship Full of Rusty Needles: How the Chinese Convinced Rajah Suran to Sail Back to India. Retold from "Sejaret Malayou." Translated by M. Devic and Chauncey C. Starkweather in *Moorish and Malayan Literature* (London: The Colonial Press, 1901), 93–121. This text may also be found online and downloaded as *Sedjaret Malayou*. Malayan Series (Cambridge, ONT: In Parenthesis Publications, 2000). http://www.yorku.ca/inpar/sedjaret_devic.pd. The *Sejaret Malayou*, also called *The Malay Annals,* was composed circa 1612 and contains both historical and fanciful matter. The retelling in this book is by Singaporean storyteller Sheila Wee. Sheila can be reached at http://www.asianstorytellingnetwork.com.

Motif(s): *.K1700 Deception through bluffing. F725 Submarine world. F133 Submarine otherworld.*

Raja Suran Dives Beneath the Sea. A magical tale. Retold from the *Sedjaret Malayou.* See above. This retelling is by Singaporean storyteller Sheila Wee. Sheila can be reached at http://www.asianstorytellingnetwork.com.

Motif(s): *F725 Submarine world. F133 Submarine otherworld. D1525 Magic submarine ship (boat).*

Badang, the Strongman of Singapura. Retold from the *Sedjaret Malayou.* See above. The version in this book is retold by Singaporean teller Kiran Shah. http://www.asianstorytellingnetwork.com

Motif(s): *F610 Remarkably strong man.*

How Malacca Got Its Name. Retold from the *Sedjaret Malayou.* See above.

Motif(s): *W32 Bravery.*

The Swordfish Attack. This tale is retold from the *Sejaret Malayou.* See above. I have left off the ending of the swordfish story. The *Sejaret Malayou* tells us that the sultan's advisors warned him that such a clever boy would be a danger when he grew up. So it was considered just that the boy be killed. After that, it is written, the city of Singapore felt the weight of the boy's blood. The tale is similar to *K771 Unicorn tricked into running horn into tree. Type 1640.*

Legends of the Sultanate of Perak

The Silver Arrow. Retold from "The Tradition" in *His Majesty Sultan Azlan Shah,* by Khao Kay Kim. (Kuala Lumpur: Pelanduk Publishing, 1991) and from "History of the Perak Sultanate" in *Lord of Kinta: The Biografi of Dato Panglima Kinta Eusoff,* by Datin Ragayah Eusoff (Kuala Lumpur: Pelanduk Publishing, 1995). Thanks to Mohd. Taib b. Mohamed, State Librarian of Perak, for this information.

> Motif(s): *D1314.1.2 Magic arrow shot to determine where to build city.*

The Legend of the White-blooded Semang Girl. Retold from *His Majesty Sultan Azlan Shah* and from *Lord of Kinta.* See above.

> Motif(s): *H41 Recognition of royalty by personal characteristics or traits.*

The Sword of Alexander the Great. Retold from *His Majesty Sultan Azlan Shah* and from *Lord of Kinta.* See above.

> Motif(s): *A1578 Origin of family ingsignia.*

The Magical Arrival of the Descendants of Alexander the Great. Retold from *His Majesty Sultan Azlan Shah* and from *Lord of Kinta.* See above.

> Motif(s): *D475.1.6 Transformation: rice to gold.*

Tales of Singapore

The Most Skilled Carpenter of Singapore. This story is retold from Yu Shouhao, *Malaiya Minjian Gushi, Vol. 2.* Translated by Yeung Ching Kong. Stith Thompson cites one tale of a barber's shaving contest, but not with a baby and not with an axe!

> Motif(s): *H500 Test of cleverness or ability. H504.2 Barber's contest in shaving (without waking man).* Thompson gives one tale, from India.

The Cat's Tail. Retold by Rosemary Somaiah from 'Kamut's Story' in *The Lion City and Other Stories from Malay Literature,* by Roy Britton (Singapore: Times Publishers, 1985). Rosemary tells stories in Singapore and can be reached at http://www.asianstorytellingnetwork.com.

> Motif(s): *A2378.4.1 Why animal has short tail.* This tale is similar to a reportedly Thai tale *MacDonald A2378.8.7* Why cat's tail has curl at end.* In this story a cat keeps its tail curled around a cup to keep anyone from poisoning the king. (In Frances Carpenter, *Wonder Tales of Cats and Dogs* [New York: Doubleday, 1955], 43–51).

Sisters Island. As told by Kiran Shah, Panna Kantilal, and Jessie Goh. This legend has been retold here by three Singapore storytellers. It is a well-known legend, and Kiran remembers picnicking on the island once. They went in a small boat to a little beach there. A lengthy version of this tale is told as "Islands of Beauty & Peace" in *Tales from the Islands of Singapore,* by Ron Chandran-Dudley (Singapore: Landmark Books, 2001), 75–94. In Chandran-Dudley's version the pirate chief appears on the island as a ghost and must tell this story in order to be released from a spell. He says he was sucked into the sea when the girls died and was cursed to tell his tale. Having told it now, he dies.

> Motif(s): *A955.10 Islands from transformed object or person.*

Mat Jenin and the Coconuts. Retold from "Mat Jenin" in Damiana L. Eugenio, *ASEAN Folk Literature* (Manila: ASEAN Committee on Culture and Information, 1995), 512–13.

> Motif(s): *J2061 Air-castle shattered by lack of forethought.*

More Malay Place Legends

The Legend of the Beautiful Mahsuri and Her Seven-generation Curse. Retold from several sources. The tale appears in *Legends of Langkawi,* by Mohamed Zahir Haji Ismail (Utusan Publications & Distributors Sdn. Bhd, 2000) and in *Myths and Legends of Malaysia,* by Pugalenthii (Singapore: V.J. Times, 2002), 33–53. The story may be found online, along with a painting of Mahsuri and a photo of her eighth-generation ancestor, at http://www.abcmalaysia.com/tour_malaysia/lgkwi_mahsuri.htm.

> Motif(s): *M474 Curse on land.*

The Origin of Lake Chini. Retold from *Folk Tales of Malaysia* by Zakaria bin Hitam. New Delhi: Learners Press, 1995, 107–124. Pictures of Lake Chini http://members. fortunecity.com/tkkhong/chini/index.htm.

> Motif(s): *A920.8.1 Lake from violating tabu.*

The Naga Dragons of Lake Chini. Retold from *Folk Tales of Malaysia,* by Zakaria bin Hitam (New Delhi: Learners Press, 1995), 107–24. A different version of the origin of Pulau Tioman is found in *Myths and Legends of Malaysia,* by Pugalenthii (Singapore: V.J. Times, 2002), 98–104. Story explains origin of Pulau Tioman and Pulau Daik from dragons' bodies.

> Motif(s): *A955.10 Islands from transformed object or person.*

The Great White Crocodile. Retold from *Folk Tales of Malaysia,* by Zakaria bin Hitam (New Delhi: Learners Press, 1995), 107–24.

> Motif(s): *B491.3 Helpful crocodile.* This resembles also tales such as *B11.11 Fight with dragon.*

The Princess of Gunong Ledang (Mount Ophir). This famous tale appears in the *Malay Annals* and has been retold in many forms. Sometimes it is said that the princess asked for a cup of the sultan's blood, sometimes for the blood of his son, sometimes for both. The old woman is often interpreted as the princess in disguise. My version is retold from "The Maid of the Mountain," in *Malayan Fables: Retold from the Malay Annals. Book I,* by Ann Parkinson (Singapore: Eastern Universities Press, Ltd., 1959), 77–81. In another version, "The Princess of Mount Ophir," in *Folk Tales of Malaysia,* by Zakaria bin Hitam (London: MacMillan, 1989), 27–35, those sent to fetch the princess are the courtiers Laksamana Hang Tuah, Sang Setia, and Tun Mamat. That tale concludes: "According to many old people in Kuala Rompin, Pahang, the Princess of Mount Ophir used to come to Lubuk Kuala Behah in the Rompin River during nights of the full moon to have the split lime bathing ceremony there. Whenever she had the ceremonial bath, thousands of fish in the river, as well as those at the river mouth, died." Mt. Ophir (Gunung Ledang) is 4,186 ft. high and is near the Johore–Malacca border.

> Motif(s): *H310 Suitor test.*

The Tidal Wave at Palembang. Retold from "The Three Ancient Kings of Sumatra," in *Malay Myths and Legends,* by Jan Knappert (Kuala Lumpur: Heinemann Educational Books (Asia) Ltd., 1980), 204–7.

> Motif(s): *D984.4 Tidal wave for breaking tabu.* Stith Thompson gives variants from the Lau Islands and from India. Given the occurrence of tidal waves in Malay seas, this tale likely was spawned by an actual event.

The Legend of Batu Gadjah. Retold from a tale sent to me by Mohd. Taib b. Mohamed of Ipoh, Perak, and Suraya Arrifin. Suraya lives at Batu Gadjah, Perak, where may be seen the elephant rock in this story. Batu (rock) Gadjah (elephant).

> This is similar to *A973 Origin of stones: punishment for discourtesy. A974 Rocks from transformation of people to stone.*

Magical Tales

The Elephant Princess. A folktale from Pattani. Retold from *Fables and Folktales from an Eastern Forest.* Collected and translated by Walter Skeat (Singapore: D.H. Moore, 1955), 38–40. This unusual tale was collected by Skeat in Pattani. Pattani is now one of the southernmost provinces of Thailand. In the province live both Malay and Thai peoples. Thus in this story the Prince has been studying at a Thai temple.

Motif(s): *D314.3 Transformation: elephant to person.* Stith Thompson gives only one source, from West Africa.

Motif(s): *B601.5 Marriage to elephant.* Stith Thompson lists only one tale, Hottentot. This tale includes motif *F959.3.4 Weapon (missile) miraculously removed from wound.* See notes for "The White Crocodile" below. In that story a man pulls a spear point from a wounded crocodile and is rewarded.

The Princess of Umbrella Hill: Puteri Bukit Payung. A folktale from Terengganu. Retold by Kamini Ramachandran.

Motif(s): *C650 The one compulsory thing.*

The Singing Top. A folktale from Perak. A version of this tale appears in *Myths and Legends of Malaysia,* by Pugalenthii (Singapore: V.J. Times, 2002), 155–61. Pulau Indera Sakti is in Perak State at the mouth of the Perak River. Singapore storyteller Kamini Ramachandran and Perak State Librarian Mohd. Taib b. Mohamed helped with details of the story. The top was said to speak *pantun,* so I have inserted *pantun* from *Flowers of the Sun: An Introduction to the Malay Pantun,* by Katharine Sim (Singapore: Eastern Universities Press, 1957).

Motif(s): *T75.3 Unrequited love expressed in song (poem). T11.1.1 Beauty of woman reported to king causes quest for her as his bride. H1381.3.1.1 Quest for bride for king (prince). Type 531.*

Ayam Jatam Berbulu Tigal: The Three-feathered Rooster. A folktale from Perlis, retold by Kamini Ramachandran. Kamini is a Singapore storyteller.

Motif(s): *B469.5 Helpful cock.*

Tales of Kancil the Mouse Deer

Many of the Kancil tales are found in the *Hikayat Pelandok Jinaka,* a Malay text the existence of which was first noted in 1736, but which scholars believe to be from the sixteenth century. The tale cycle is discussed in *A History of Classical Malay Literature,* by Sir Richard Windstedt (Petaling Jaya: Malaysian Branch of the Royal Asiatic Society, 1992). The Mouse Deer tales have been retold in many English-language children's books. For collections see Margueritte Harmon Bro, *How Mouse Deer Became King* (Garden City, NY: Doubleday, 1966) and Harold Courlander, *Kantchil's Lime Pit and Other Stories from Indonesia* (New York: Harcourt, Brace, 1950). Kancil is the lesser mouse deer (*tragulus javanicus*), also called a chevrotain.

Kancil and Sang Buwaya. *Buwaya* means "crocodile." "Sang Buwaya" is a respectful way to address the crocodile.

> *MacDonald motif K579.2.1* Kantchil (mouse deer) takes census of crocodiles, crossing stream on their back.* A similar story is also told in Japan, in which a white hare plays the same trick.

Also in this story is *K543 Biting the foot. Fox to bear, who is biting his foot: "You are biting the tree root." Bear lets loose.* Stith Thompson cites variants of this tale from Indonesia, Malaysia, Brazil, Georgia, the West Indies, and South Africa. *Type 5 Biting the Foot* cites many European variants, Turkish, West Indian, Indian (22), and African (16). *MacDonald K543.0.1* Kantchil (or jackal) to crocodile who is biting his foot. "You are biting a tree root"* gives variants from Pakistan and Bangladesh as well as from Indonesia and Malaysia. *Motif K607.2 Crocodile masking as log obeys suggestion that he move upstream (sink). He thus betrays himself.* This is a variation on *K607.2 The cave call. ("Hello, house!") An animal suspecting the presence of an enemy in his cave (house), calls.* The animal is tricked into answering, thus revealing itself. This tale appears in Latin America, the Caribbean, and as a Brer Rabbit tale from the American South. It is also in the Indian Panchatantra.

I can't trace the actual source of my own retelling because I began telling this while living in Singapore in 1969, basing my tale on various English and Malay texts available to me there. A recent picture book version is *Kancil and the Crocodiles: A Tale from Malayasia,* by Noreha Yussof Day (New York: Simon & Schuster, 1996). The tale appears in Bro (22–28) and Courlander (87–94) and in Adéle De Leeuw's *Indonesian Legends and Folktales* (New York: Nelson, 1961), 77–80.

Kancil and Sang Harimau. The tale appears in Adéle De Leeuw, *Indonesian Legends and Folktales* (New York: Nelson, 1961), 68–74. My version was created in 1969 while telling stories in Singapore.

The story contains several motifs: *K1111.0.1.1 Dupe wishing to learn to play flute puts tongue in split bamboo.* This is related to *K1111 Dupe puts hand (paws) into cleft of tree. Type 38* cites numerous European versions, plus Native American, Puerto Rican, Indian, and Brer Rabbit. *K1023.1 Dupe allowed to guard (play) "king's drum": it is a wasp's nest.* In a similar Brer Rabbit tale from the American South, hare tells fox that a wasp's nest is a clump of grapes. In a Mexican tale, hare tells coyote that a hornet's nest is a school bell. *K1023.1.1 Dupe allowed to guard "king's girdle": it is a snake.*

Kancil and the Big Hole. In some variants, Kancil tricks the Giant Gergasi into the pit in order to catch him. This is a variant of *Type 31 The Fox Climbs from the Pit on the Wolf's Back (K652),* which has many European and Indian variants. *MacDonald K652.1 Kantchil persuades animals to come down in pit for safety at end of the world.*

The tale appears in Margueritte Harmon Bro, *How Mouse Deer Became King* (Garden City, NY: Doubleday, 1966), 72–78; Harold Courlander, *Kantchil's Lime Pit and Other Stories from Indonesia* (New York: Harcourt, Brace, 1950), 6–10; and Adéle De Leeuw's *Indonesian Legends and Folktales* (New York: Nelson, 1961), 77–80.

Kancil and the Otter's Babies. Retold from: "A Tale by the Wayside," in *In Malay Forests,* by Sir George Maxwell (Singapore: Eastern Universities Press, 1957), 178–83. First published in Penang in 1907. Maxwell says of this story, "I heard it one day when we were resting in the forest near Teluk Kepaiang after a deer drive." His Malay hunting friends told the story. Maxwell points out that such stories are far more than just children's amusements and can be referred to in the village council when important matters are under discussion. Of this story of the otter's babies he says "many years ago it was told at length in the Perak State Council and a very important decision was based upon it."

This is a variant of *Z49.6 Trial among the animals. Deer steps on kitten: cat investigates. Deer has been frightened by bird . . . ,* etc. Stith Thompson gives sources from Indonesia, Malaysia, the Philippines, and India. MacDonald adds variants from Burma, the West Indies, China, and Africa. A well-known variant is *Why Mosquitoes Buzz in People's Ears,* by Verna Aardema (New York: Dial, 1975).

Fables about Plants

A Fight Among the Vegetables. Retold from *Fables and Folktales from an Eastern Forest.* Collected and translated by Walter Skeat (Singapore: D.H. Moore, 1955), 13–15. Skeat tells us that this was taken down "on the banks of the Upper Tembeling River in the interior of Pahang." Skeat collected his tales " during the progress of the Cambridge Expedition of 1899 through the remoter States of the Malay Peninsula." In a Bidayuh tale from Sarawak, the vegetables are again arguing about who is the best staple. The Great Spirit lines them all up and lets humans choose. Job's Tears, which has been hollering and beating its chest, saying it is best of all, is chosen as least popular by humans for a staple food. At this Job's Tears jumps down from the meeting place and falls so hard on the ground that its chest is bashed in. For this reason, and because it was beating its chest earlier, Job's tears are concave on all sides. And they are used only for making fermented drinks and preserving pickled fish, not as a staple of the diet. "Job's Tears" told by Arthur Atos Langgi of Kampung Ta'ee, Serian in *King Siliman and Other Bidayuh Folk Tales.* Compiled by Robert Sulis Ridu, Ritikos Jitab, and Jonas Noeb. Dayak Studies (Kota Samarahan: Universiti Malaysia Sarawak, 2001), 61–64.

Motif(s): *A2720 Plant characteristics as punishment.*

Gelugur and Jelutung. Retold from "Gelugur Jelutung," in *A Tale a Day: December,* by Othman Puteh and Aripid Said. Translated by Sudanda, from *Himpunan 366 Cerita Rakyat Malaysia, 1995* (Kuala Lumpur, Malaysia: Utusan Publications, 1998), 18.

Motif(s): *A1471.1 Origin of trade between two places.*

Cloves for the Breath. Retold from "The Clove," in *A Tale a Day: December,* by Othman Puteh and Aripid Said. Translated by Sudanda, from *Himpunan 366 Cerita Rakyat Malaysia, 1995* (Kuala Lumpur, Malaysia: Utusan Publications, 1998), 18.

> Motif(s): *A2663 Origin of clove.*

Humorous Malay Tales: Pak Pandir and Other Foolish Fellows

Pak Pandir and Pak Kadok are stock foolish characters in Malay folklore. For more Pak Pandir stories, see "Pak Pandir, the Village Fool," in *Malaysian Children's Favourite Stories,* by Kay Lyons. Illustrated by Marin Loh (Boston: Tuttle Publishing, 2004). A recent book for adults drawing on these themes is *Eh! Wat You Talking? Chronicles of Malay Humor,* by Syed Ali Tawfik Al-attas (MPH Group Publishing, 2007). In Malay a good collection is *Cherita Jenaka,* by Raja Haji Yahya (Kuala Lumpur: Oxford University Press, 1963). The text is from Perak, written before 1908. It includes tales of Pak Kadok, Pak Pandir, Lebai Malang, Pak Belalang, and Si-Luncai. Jan Knappert's *Malay Myths and Legends* (Kuala Lumpur: Heinemann, 1980) also contains tales of Pak Pandir, Lebai Malang, Pak Bilalang, and Si-Luncai.

Lending the Water Buffalo. Retold from *Dewan English Readers: Book Eleven* (Kuala Lumpur: Dewan Bahasa Dan Pustaka, Ministry of Education, Federation of Malaya, 1963).

> Motif(s): *MacDonald J1552.1.1 Loans refused. The ass is not at home. A man wants to borrow an ass. The owner says that the ass is not at home. The ass brays and the borrower protests. "Will you believe an ass and not a graybeard like me?"* MacDonald cites Spanish, Turkish (Hodja), and Saudi Arabian variants.

Pak Pandir and Pak Kadok Go Shopping. Retold from *Dewan English Readers: Book Eleven* (Kuala Lumpur: Dewan Bahasa Dan Pustaka, Ministry of Education, Federation of Malaya, 1963).

> Motif(s): *K1082 Ogres (large animals) duped into fighting each other. Trickster strikes one so that he thinks the other has done it. Type 1640.*

Pak Pandir and the Giant Gergasi. Retold by Singapore storyteller Kamini Ramachandran.

> Motif(s): *G520 Ogre deceived into self-injury. Type 328.*

Part 3: Tales from the Ethnic Peoples of Borneo

Tales from Sabah

The Terrible Karambau. From Yunis Rojiin Gabu, Kota Kinabalu, April 2003. She learned it from her grandmother, Gunih Rampasan. Told to Margaret Read MacDonald and Nat and Jen Whitman en route to Kota Kinabalu after rural library storytellings.

> Motif(s): *G550 Rescue from Ogre*. European tales tell of a captured boy given to the Giant's wife to cook. And of her attempts to fatten him. The digging help of the mouse and bubut bird is unique to this tale.

The Rolling Red-eyed Head. From Yunis Rojiin Gabu, Kota Kinabalu, April 2003. She learned it from her grandmother, Gunih Rampasan. Told to Margaret Read MacDonald and Nat and Jen Whitman en route to Kota Kinabalu after rural library storytellings.

> Motif(s): *R261.1 Pursuit by rolling head*. Stith Thompson cites Native American, South American Indian, African, and Japanese tales. And Thompson cites Seneca, Caviña, Tumpasa, and Aruaucanian tales of *G361.2 Great head as ogre*. Giant rolling vegetables appear now and then in folklore. In a tale from Upper Volta a giant pumpkin cut by a boy chases him, smashes all in its path, is split by horned sheep and becomes two pieces, earth and sky. (*MacDonald A641.3* Giant pumpkin, Feegba, chases boy who cuts it.*) *MacDonald R261.2* Pursuit by rolling gourd. Old woman pursued by green gourd she cuts. Animals fail to stop it, but bear sits on and squashes.* This tale is in Richard Chase's *Grandfather Tales* (213–21) and as a picture book *The Green Gourd,* by Tony Johnston (Putnam, 1992). From Zanzibar comes a tale of a rolling giant pumpkin growing from spot where ogre died, *Bimwili and the Zimwi,* by Verna Aardema (Dial, 1985). And an Anansi story from Jamaica shows Anansi being pursued by yams angry at having been dug up. See "Ticky-Picky Boom Boom," in Philip Sherlock, *West Indian Folk-Tales* (Walck, 1966), 76–83.

The Girl Who Was Kidnapped by an Orangutan. From Yunis Rojiin Gabu, Kota Kinabalu, August 2005. She learned it from her grandmother, Gunih Rampasan. Told to Margaret Read MacDonald at Sabah State Library.

> The orangutan in this story functions as an ogre: *G352 Wild beast as ogre. G501 Stupid Ogre.* The tender grooming scenes in the nest make the tale begin to resemble *D735.1 Beauty and the Beast.* But in the end she is only tricking him to escape. *G550 Escape from ogre.* The patient weaving of the escape rope through grooming is a delightful motif.

The Fairy Bride. From Yunis Rojiin Gabu, Kota Kinabalu, August 2005. She learned it from her grandmother, Gunih Rampasan. Told to Margaret Read MacDonald at Sabah State Library.

Motif(s): *F302.6 Fairy mistress leaves man when he breaks tabu. C31.9 Tabu: revealing secrets of supernatural wife.* Stith Thompson lists many tales of offending supernatural wives: European, African, Indian, Japanese, Maori, Melanesian, and Native American. A common supernatural wife motif is that of the fairy whose wings (or clothes) are stolen. *MacDonald F302.4.2.1 Fairy comes into man's power when he steals her clothes* gives Greek, Eskimo, Yoruban, Scottish, Chinese, Burmese, Colombian, and Native American variants. *MacDonald & Sturm F302.4.2+* cites Inuit, Chukchi, Irish, Korean, and Welsh variants. In the well-known Thai tale of Muang Lap Lai (the land of beautiful women), the husband looses his wife when he lies to his young son (Supaporn Vathanprida, *Thai Tales,* Libraries Unlimited, 1994). It is most unusual for the wronged wife to be regained by the husband. The grueling overnight ordeal in our Kadazan tale, in which the man follows the rolling python with his son in its grasp, is amazing.

Stealing Fruit: Two Dusun Puzzle Tales. Retold from "Some Dusun Fables," by Ivor H. N. Evans, *The Sarawk Museum Journal* 5 (New Series) (July 1955). (Kuching, Sarawak: Sarawak Government Printing Office, 1955), 245–47.

The first tale is *K341 Owner's interest distracted while goods are stolen. Type 15.* The clever sewing together of leaves to weigh down the tree seems a unique motif.

The Python Husband. Retold by Margaret Read MacDonald from *Totunod Sungai/ Tombonuwo. Cerita Dongeng Sungai/Tombonuwo Sungai/Tombonuwo Folk Tales.* Sabah Folk Tales No. 4. Compiled by John Wayne King and Julie K. King. Story was told by Kopunti Bte Komangsi (Kota Kinabalu: Department of Sabah Museum and State Archives, 1990). Kopunti bte Komangsi was a grandmother from Kuala Lingkabau, Sugut, a village along the Sugut river. The tale was recorded in Sungai and translated into English by the collectors, John Wayne King and Julie K. King. The version given here has been developed for storytelling by Margaret Read MacDonald. A tale of a girl who married a snake was told to MacDonald and Nat and Jen Whitman during a visit to a Sungai village in 2003, but the ending was different.

Motif(s): This is an unusual variant of *D735.1 Beauty and the Beast Type 425 C.*

MacDonald D735.1 includes variants from France (beast), Ireland (bear), Slovenia (bear), Spain (bear), Italy (wizard), Brittany (snake), Philippines (monkey), and gypsies (dog). A comparison with the British variant *The Great, Smelly, Slobbery, Small-Tooth Dog,* retold by Margaret Read MacDonald (August House, 2007) shows the following similarities: single parent; girl agrees reluctantly to go with dog/snake; distant travel; fine house; fine food provided; dog/snake turns to man; wed. The python story, however, differs from the "Beauty and the Beast" motif in motive. The snake becomes a man, not because she shows him love, but because she discovers his skin.

Motif(s): *D721.3 Disenchantment by destroying skin (covering). Type 423, 430, 440, 441.* Stith Thompson cites this motif from Iceland, Turkey, India, China, Korea, as well as Eskimo, Indonesian, Native American, South American Indian, and African. MacDonald and Sturm cite variants from Brittany, Germany, India, Latvia, Mexico, Russia, China, and Vietnam. This is also *B641 Marriage to person in beast form.* Mac-Donald cites a Latvian version in which a hedgehog turns into a prince when his skin is burnt. And in an Indian version of *D861.1 Magic object stolen by host (at inn)* a jackal becomes a prince when his skin is burned.

Amazingly, there is a very similar tale from the Wai Wai people of the Amazon. In their tale a girl and her mother live in a house raised on pillars beside a river. While at the river, the girl looks directly at a bathing man and their eyes lock. It turns out that he is a snake person in human form at that moment. That night, when she and her mother are alone in the house, the snake comes with all of his snake people. He calls for her to come down and marry him. She refuses repeatedly. So he calls the giant armadillo to dig a tunnel from the river and flood out the house. The girl and her mother are trapped in the house with rising waters. However the ending of the tale is different. Dawn breaks and the snake people leave. The wai-wai tale is in *Xingu. The Indians and Their Myths,* by Orlando Villas Boas and Cláudio Villas Boas (New York: Farrar, Straus & Giroux, 1973), 77–79.

The White Crocodile. As told by Abdul Rahman Bulinti Lindas of Kampong Butu Putih, on the Kinabatangan River, Sabah. See for discussion of story telling event.

Motif(s): *B622.2 Crocodile as wooer.* Stith Thompson cites one variant from India. *F127.3 Journey to land of crocodiles.* The tale's climactic moment, in which the hero pulls a stake from the side of the crocodile king (*F959.3.4 Weapon [missile] miraculously removed from wound*), is very like a moment in a Tlingit tale that I heard in 1960 in Hoonah, Alaska. In that tale the hero pulls a spear from the side of the sea otter chief after having been taken underwater to the sea lions' cave. *MacDonald & Sturm *A2135.5 Origin of killer whale.* See Tlingit tale in Mary L. Beck, *Heroes and Heroines in Tlingit-Haida Legend* (Anchorage: Northwest Books, 1989), 1–7. *B380 Animal grateful for relief from pain.*

A different version of this tale is "Sebilit Bilit and Terunggari," in *Animal Tales of Sabah,* by P. S. Shim (Kota Kinabalu: Natural History Publications [Borneo], 2002), 54–55. In that tale a little girl is eaten by Terunggari, the giant white crocodile who lives in the Kinabatangan River. Her mother, Sebilit Bilit, follows and stabs him with a spear made of a bamboo. Later his grandchildren come to beg her to remove the stake and she does, on condition that he swear never to eat her descendants. Say to the crocs, "Do not eat me because I am a descendant of Sebilit Bilit." A similar tale, this time from the Murut people, is also given in *Animal Tales of Sabah.* In "Crocodiles of the River Sook," a crocodile chokes on the porcupine quill hairpin of a woman he has eaten. A croc begs an old woman, Adutor, to come help, and carries her to the crocs' cave on his back. After she has removed the quill, she is kept for a long time in the cave but finally begs to go home. The crocs promise never to eat another Murut and she promises that her people will not molest crocodiles. To this day the Murut do not kill crocodiles. In "The King of the Crocodiles," in *Malaysian Children's Favorite Stories,* by Kay Lyons (Rutland, VT: Tuttle, 2004), 37–43, a crocodile in human form asks Bangsat to remove a fishbone from his daughter's throat, turns into King of Crocodiles and carries B. on back, gives gold. Not to tell. Tells village chief, Tabiko. T. tries to trick croc king into marrying son to his daughter. Crocs bring much gold as dowry; box to hold it has hole in bottom and is thus never filled. Crocs discover trick; eat everyone except Bangsat. Wage war on humans to this day. No ethnic source is cited for this tale.

See also "Mang Aloi Visits the Monkey People" in the section "Tales from Sarawak" in Part 3 of this book, in which a monkey is healed by a human visitor.

The Origin of Leeches. Told by Abdul Rahman Bulinti Lindas of Kampong Batu Putih, on the Kinabatangan River, Sabah, April 2003. This tale is not specific to the Sungai. A Kadazan version appears as "The Origin of Land and Water Leeches," in *Kadazan Folklore,* by Rita Lasimbang (Kota Kinabalu: National History Publications [Borneo] in association with Kadazandusun Language Foundation, 1999), 22–25. The book also contains a story of a woman who suckles a caterpillar, which grows larger and larger. It calls out "Wa-ong!" whenever it wants to be nursed, and the woman hurries to feed the caterpillar. Eventually it becomes as big as a pillow and the husband hacks it with his parang. The wife is released from the caterpillar's spell. These two tales are collected from the Panampang district of Sabah from Zandi' Rosina Sogondu-Lasimbang of Kampung Nampasin. The tale also appears as "A Family in Search of Children," in *Tongo Tangon Kadazan Labuk-Kinabatangan/Cerita Dongeng Kadazan Labuk-Kinabatangan/Labuk-Kinabatangan Kadazan Folk Tales. Sabah Folk Tales, No 1.,* by Hope M. Hurlbut (Kota Kinabalu: Department of Sabah Museum, 1992), 36. The tale was collected by Matius Matuland of Kampung Wonod, Labuk-Kinabatangan district.

A2435.6.3 Why leech feeds on human blood. Stith Thompson gives one variant, from India. *A2182.2 Origin of leech.* This is reminiscent of Northwest Coast and Eskimo tales in which the chief's daughter adopts a worm. *MacDonald F911.6.2* Chief's daughter feeds pet worm. It becomes devouring dragon.* Eskimo tale in Helen Caswell, *Shadows from the Singing House* (Rutland, VT: Tuttle, 1968), 88–92. *MacDonald & Sturm F911.6.4* Young woman secluded during puberty rituals grows lonely. Men put woodworm near her to scare her, she takes it as a pet, nurses it and it grows huge.* Tlingit tale in Mary L. Beck, *Heroes and Heroines in Tlingit-Haida Legend* (Anchorage: Northwest Books, 1989), 91–97. There is also a Bolivian tale of a woman who keeps a giant worm as a child. It grows enormously until it leaves for the sky and becomes the Milky Way. In Patricia Aldana's *Jade and Iron* (Toronto: Douglas and McIntyre, 1996).

Why Dog Is Treated Well. Retold from "A Dog's Life," in *Animal Tales of Sabah,* by P. S. Shim (Kota Kinabalu: Natural History Publications [Borneo], 2002), 10–11. A Murut tale told by Sibah Lee.

Tales from Sarawak

The Squirrel and the Forest Gecko. Retold from "The Squirrel and the Forest Gecko," by Tugang Sugun, from Long Jek, Seping, Belaga, in *Suket: Penan Folk Stories.* Dayak Studies. Compiled by Jayl Langub (Koto Samarahan: Universiti Malaysia Sarawak, 2001), 29–33. Tugang Sugun was headman of Long Jek on the Seping River, Belaga, when he told this story. He was in his mid-sixties at the time.

> Motif(s): *W152 Stinginess. A2238 Animal characteristics: punishment for greed.*

The Liar's Pile. Retold from: *Iban Stories,* by Heidi Munan (Kuala Lumpur: Penerbit Fajar Bakti Sdn. Bhd., 1990), 14–20. The introduction tells us that this book is based on tales written down by an Iban teacher who heard them from her mother. It is not clear whether or not the author is this teacher.

> Motif(s): *Q263 Lying (perjury) punished.*

Protecting the Forests of Tanjung Tamelan. Retold from "The Gun of Tanjung Tamelan," in *Iban Folktales,* by Heini Munan. (Kuala Lumpur: Penerbit Fajar Bakti Sdn. Bhd., 1990), 25–35. Written by an Iban teacher whose mother told her these stories.

Mang Aloi Visits the Monkey People. This story was told in 1955 by R. Nyadoh, a Land Dayak man from Tapuh, Serian. He told it as a historical account of Kampong Libur near Serian. In 1955, when this story was told, Dingun Lidang was head chief at Kampong Libur near Serian. The jar mentioned in the story was kept by his father, Rapak. Retold from "The Monkey Men and the Jar of Gold," by R. Nyadoh, in *The Sarawak Museum Journal* 5 (New Series) (July 1955) (Kuching, Sarawak: Sarawak Government Printing Office, 1955), 310–13.

> This tale appears in other Asian countries. The stories from Japan and China cited below are quite similar. A man, keeping very still, is transported to the monkey's country. He returns with treasure. A second man imitates him, fails to keep still, and is dropped. *MacDonald J2415.23* Farmer disguised as scarecrow taken as Jizo statue by monkeys* cites two Japanese sources for this tale. For a version told by the Dai people, the Thai Lue of Yunan, China, see "The Big Man Drum," in *Shake-it-up Tales!*, by Margaret Read MacDonald (August House, 2000), 75–80. The Dyak tale, however, adds the motif of healing the monkey grandmother, for which the hero is given a reward. A similar motif appears in a Sungai tale from Sabah in which the hero heals a crocodile king. See "The White Crocodile."

> Motif(s): *Q94 Reward for cure.*

Tales from Brunei

The Dollarbird and the Short-tailed Monkey. Retold from *Dusun Folktales: A Collection of Eighty-eight Folktales in the Dusun Language of Brunei with English Translations*. Compiled and translated by Eva Maria Kershaw. Southeast Asia Paper No. 39 (Honolulu: Center for Southeast Asian Studies, School of Hawaiian, Asian, and Pacific Studies, University of Hawaii, 1994).

A somewhat different Kadazan version from Sabah is given as "Tompii," in *Kadazan Folklore,* by Rita Lasimbang (Kota Kinabalu: Natural History Publications [Borneo], 1999), 10–15. In this tale the Tompii' bird plans to sing to bring rain during a drought, but the bigger birds mock it so that it leaves Borneo. Butterfly brings it back and it calls the rain. Today smaller birds always band together and chase off large birds, remembering how cruel the big birds were to Tompii'. In an Iban story, "The Fable of Burong Pong-Kapong," the *Pong-Kapong* birds emigrate to Sumatera because the Juak fish bites their baby's leg. It was these birds who called the fruit. So butterfly and fruit fly agree to go fetch them back (after other animals offer excuses). They float there on a piece of wood. The birds return and build a nest on Mount Kinabalu. But they still fear the *Juak* fish. The *Juak* fish promises not to harm anyone again if folks pay it respect. The birds stay, and every year, after the rains, they make their call and the trees blossom and bear fruit (*Iban Stories,* by Heidi Munan. Kuala Lumpur: Penerbit Fajar Bakti Sdn. Bhd., 1990, 6–13). A Penan version was collected from Balan Balang of Long Bee, Silat, Baram, and appears as "Kangkaput," in *Suket: Penan Folk Stories*. Dayak Studies. Compiled by Jayl Langub (Koto Samarahan: Universiti Malaysia Sarawak, 2001), 18–23. In this version *Kangkaput* refuses to go back with butterfly, but asks dove to take care of the eggs she left behind on Borneo. The young who hatched would be able to call to make the trees fruit. But the *Buleng* fish, who bit her, cannot have any.

The sequence of animals who fail to fetch the Dollarbird reminds us of the train of animals who attempt to bring up the earth in the Native American *A812 Earth diver* motif. Likewise many Native American *A1414 Origin of Fire* tales feature strings of animals that attempt to bring back fire and fail, often bearing a mark of their failure.

The King of the Mosquitoes. Retold from "The King of the Mosquitoes," in Damiana L. Eugenio, *ASEAN Folk Literature* (Manila: ASEAN Committee on Culture and Information, 1995), 408–11.

Q2.1 Kind and unkind girls. Type 480. This is one of the most widely distributed folktales in world literature. MacDonald gives variants from England, Ireland, Norway, Sweden, France, Italy, Switzerland, Germany, Russia, Poland, Estonia, Latvia, Greece, Bulgaria, Serbia, Czechoslovakia, Appalachia, Venezuela, Haiti, South Africa, West Africa, Sierra Leone, India, Ceylon, Japan, and Burma. MacDonald and Sturm add variants for Chile, African American, India, Benin, and Siberia.

Dayang Bongsu and the Crocodile. Retold from "Dayang Bongsu and the Crocodile," in *Dusun Folktales: A Collection of Eighty-Eight Folktales in the Dusun Language of Brunei with English Translations.* Compiled and Translated by Eva Maria Kershaw. Southeast Asia Paper No 39 (Honolulu: Center for Southeast Asian Studies, School of Hawaiian, Asian and Pacific Studies, University of Hawaii, n.d.), 180–86. The story continues with other adventures and ends with the monkey finding a husband for Dayang Bongsu. In a second story in this collection Dayang Bongsu, a youngest child abandoned by her sisters, is looked after by a monkey who finds her a husband.

    D1611 Magic object answers for fugitive. Left behind to impersonate fugitive and delay pursuit. B622.2 Crocodile as wooer.

Si Perawai, the Greedy Fisherman. Retold from "Si Perawai, the Greedy Fisherman," in Damiana L. Eugenio, *ASEAN Folk Literature* (Manila: ASEAN Committee on Culture and Information, 1995), 227–28.

    J2061 Air-castle shattered by lack of forethought.

Part 4: Proverbs and Pantun

Dusun Proverbs. These proverbs are selected from "Some Dusun Proverbs and Proverbial Sayings," by Ivor H. N. Evans. *The Sarawk Museum Journal* 5 (New Series) (July 1955) (Kuching, Sawarak: Sarawak Government Printing Office, 1955). They were collected from Kahung Saraiyoh on the Tempasuk (Kedamaian) River, "twenty-eight miles by bridle path from Kota Belud."

Malay Proverbs. The Malay proverbs were selected from *Malay Proverbs,* by Sir Richard Winstedt (London: John Murray, 1950).

Malay Pantun. Pantun were taken from *Flowers of the Sun: A Simple Introduction to the Enjoyment of the Pantun,* by Katharine Sim (Singapore: Eastern Universities Press, 1957). And from "The Pantun," in *A History of Classical Malay Literature,* by Sir Richard Winstedt (Petaling Jaya: The Malaysian Branch of the Royal Asiatic Society, 1992), 36–146.

Part 5: Malaysian Children's Songs and Games

    All three of the songs given here can be heard at various Web sites. Just Google the song name.

Bangau o Bangau/Egret o Egret. Text from Doretty Sikuat, Kota Kinabalu, Sabah. Tune from recording made of Doretty Sikuat singing at Sabah State Library, 2006.

Burung Kaka Tua/Old Sister Cockatoo. Sung to me by Sheila Wee, Kiran Shah, and Kamini Ramachandran in Singapore, April 2007.

Enjit Enjit Semut/Step, Step Ant. Sung and performed for me by Kamini Ramachandran, Kiran Shah, and Sheila Wee, Singapore, April 2007. Also in *Ruisi Berirama* (Singapore: National Library Board, n.d.).

APPENDIX B: MORE BOOKS TO READ

Bro, Margueritte. *How Mouse Deer Became King*. Garden City, NY: Doubleday, 1966.

Bunanta, Murti. *Indonesian Folktales*. Westport, CT: Libraries Unlimited, 2003

Courlander, Harold. *Katchil's Lime Pit, and Other Stories from Indonesia*. New York: Harcourt, Brace, 1950.

Day, Noreha Yussof. *Kancil and the Crocodiles: A Tale from Malaysia*. New York: Simon & Schuster, 1996.

DeLeeuw, Adéle. *Indonesian Legends and Folk Tales*. New York: Nelson, 1963.

Lyons, Kay. *Malaysian Children's Favourite Stories*. Rutland, VT: Tuttle, 2004.

Spagnoli, Kathy. *Kantjil and Tiger: A Tale from Indonesia*. Bothell, WA: Wright Group, 1995.

Taylor, Di. *Singapore Children's Favourite Stories*. Illustrated by L. K. Tay-Audouard. Singapore: Periplus, 2003.

APPENDIX C:
SOURCES CONSULTED

Apai Alui Becomes a Shaman and Other Iban Comic Tales/Apai Alui Nyadi Manang Enggau Ensera Iban Bukai. Compiled by Clifford Sathre. Dayak Studies. Oral Literature Series, No. 3. Kuching: Universiti Malaysia Sarawak, 2001.

Brooks, Margaret M. *North Borneo Folk Stories.* Borneo Literature Bureau, 1961.

Cerita Dongeng Sabah. Tutunungon-Tutunungon Ru Tuu-Lair Rali/Cerita Dongeng Timugon/ Timugon Folktales. Sabah Museum Booklet No. 2, 1995.

Chandran-Dudley, Ron. *Tales from the Islands of Singapore.* Singapore: Landmark Books, 2001.

Chong, Benedict S. *Tales of Borneo.* Perak: Penerbit Sanmin Sdn. Bhd, 1993.

Dentan, Robert Knox. "Enduring Scars: Cautionary Tales Among the Senoi Semai, a Peaceable People of West Malaysia." In *Traditional Storytelling Today*, edited by Margaret Read MacDonald, 130–33. Chicago: Fitzroy-Dearborn, 1999.

Dewan English Readers. Book Eleven. Kuala Lumpur: Dewan Bahasa Dan Pustaka. Ministry of Education. Federation of Malaya, 1963.

Dewan English Readers. Book Ten. Kuala Lumpur: Dewan Bahasa Dan Pustaka. Ministry of Education. Federation of Malaya, 1963. (Kantchil variants)

Dusun Folktales: Eighty-Eight Folktales in The Dusun Language of Brunei with English Translations. Compiled and translated by Eva Maria Kershaw. Southeast Asia Paper No. 39. Honolulu: Center for Southeast Asian Studies, School of Hawaiian, Asian and Pacific Studies, University of Hawai'i at Manoa, 1994.

Ebi, Ahmad. *Bidayuh Folk Tales.* Kuching: Gaya Media Sdn. Bhd., 1997.

Eng, Chuah Guat. *Tales from the Baram River.* Kuala Lumpur: Utusan Publications, 2001. From Miri, collected by Bishop pre-1970 from Kenyah people.

Folktales of Southeast Asia. Singapore: Landmark Books, 2001.

Groeneveldt, W. P. *Notes on the Malay Archipelago and Malacca.* Compiled from Chinese sources. Batavia, 1876.

Guranathan, K., ed. *Popular Malaysian Folk Tales*. Selangor: Adlaunch (Malaysia) Sdn. Bhd., 1993.

Hitam, Z. *Folk Tales of Malaysia*. London: Macmillan Publishers, 1989.

Hitam, Zakaria bin. *Folk Tales of Malaysia*. New Delhi: Learner's Press, 1995. Different text from Macmillan edition above.

Ismail, Mohamed Zahir Haji. *The Legends of Langkawi*. Kuala Lumpur: Utusan Publications and Distributors Sdn. Bhd., 2000.

Lain-Lain, Mohammad Shahidan dan. *Koleksi Repilih Cerita Rakyat Malaysia*. Kuala Lumpur: Dewan Bahasa dan Pustaka. Kementerian Pendidikan Malaysia, 1994.

Lasimbang, Rita. *Kadazan Folklore*. Kota Kinabalu: Natural History Publications (Borneo)/Kadazandusun Language Foundation, 1999.

Liton Ida'an/Cerita Dongeng Ida/an/Idā'an Folk Tales. Sabah Folk Tales No. 6. Compiled by David C. Moody. Kota Kinabalu: Department of Sabah Museum, 1993.

Lyons, Kay. *Malaysian Children's Favourite Stories*. Rutland, VT: Tuttle, 2004.

Majikol, Elsie, and Suzie Majikol. *Monsopiead: The Kadazan Warrior*. Penampang: Kadazandusun Language Foundation, 2000.

Malayan Literature: Comprising Romantic Tales, Epic Poetry and Royal Chronicles. Translated into English for the first time, with a special introduction by Chauncey C. Starkweather. Colonial Press, 1901. [Bound with *Moorish Literature*]. (Title: *Moorish and Malayan Literature*. Lamb Publishing Company. [no date]).

Marsh, Ignatia Olim. *Tales and Traditions from Sabah*. Kota Kinabalu: The Sabah Society, 1988.

Maxwell, Sir George. *In Malay Forests*. Singapore: Eastern Universities Press, 1960.

McHugh, N. J. *Hantu Hantu: An Account of Ghost Belief in Modern Malaya*. Singapore: Donald Moore, 1955.

Munan, Heidi. *Iban Stories*. Kuala Lumpur: Penerbit Fajar Bakti Sdn. Bhd., 1990.

———. *Sarawak Stories: Bidayuh and Melanau Tales*. Kuala Lumpur: Penerbit Fajar Bakti Sdn. Bhd., 1991.

———. *Stories from Sarawak: Bidayuh Stories*. Kuala Lumpur, Utusan Publications, 2005.

Myths and Legends of Singapore. Singapore: VJ Times, 1991.

Nais, Temenggŏng Datuk William. *The Hole in the Caved-in Beach (Land Dayak Stories)*. Compiled by Temenggŏng Datuk William Nais (English and Dayak Bidayuh Version). Kuching: Sarawak Literary Society, 1987.

Nana nu Rahu nu Murut Tahol/Cerita Dongeng Murut Tagal/Tagal Murut Folk Tales. Compiled by Mariann Nygren. Sabah Folk Tales No. 5. Kota Kinabalu: Department of Sabah Museum and State Archives, 1991.

Ninotaziz. *From the Written Stone: An Anthology of Malaysian Folklore*. Kuala Lumpur, Utusan Publications, 2006.

Osman, Mohd. Taib. *Bunga Rampai: Aspects of Malay Cultures*. Kuala Lumpur: Dewan Bahasa Dan Pustaka Kementerian Pendidikan Malaysia, 1988.

———. "The Tradition of Storytelling in Malaysia." In *Traditional Storytelling Today*, edited by Margaret Read MacDonald, 138–41. Chicago: Fitzroy-Dearborn, 1999.

Papers Relating to Trengganu. MBRAS REPRINT No. 10. MBRAS, 1983. Previously published as *JMBRAS* XXII, pt. 3 (June 1949).

Parkinson, Ann. *Malayan Fables. Retold from the Malay Annals by Ann Parkinson. Book I*. Singapore: Eastern Universities Press, 1956.

———. *Malayan Fables. Retold from the Malay Annals by Ann Parkinson. Book II*. Singapore: Eastern Universities Press, 1956.

Rubenstein, Carol. *The Honey Tree Song: Poems and Chants of Sarawak Dayaks*. Athens: Ohio University Press, 1985.

———. *The Nightbird Sings*. Thornhill, Dumfriesshire, Scotland: Tynron Press, 1990.

Sandin, Benedict. *The Living Legends: Borneans Telling Their Tales*. Kuala Lumpur: Dewan Bahasa dan Pustaka Malaysia, Cawangan Sarawak, Kementerian Pelajaran Malaysia, 1980.

The Sarawak Museum Journal. Issued by the Museum, Kuning, Sarawak. July 1955; July–December 1961; July–December 1962; July–December 1970; July–December 1971; July–December 1975.

Shim, P. S. *A Cultural Heritage of North Borneo: Animal Tales of Sabah*. Kota Kinabalu: Natural History Publications (Borneo), 2002.

Sim, Katharine. *Flowers of the Sun: An Introduction to the Malay Pantun*. Singapore: Eastern Universities Press, 1957.

Skeat, William. *Fables and Folk Tales from an Eastern Forest*. Cambridge, 1901.

———. *Malay Magic: Being an introduction to the folk-lore and popular religion of the Malay Peninsula*. London: Macmillan, 1900.

Sukĕt: Penan Folk Stories/ Suket Penan. Compiled by Jayl Langub. Dayak Studies. Oral Literature Series, no. 2. Kuching: University Malysia Sarawak, 2001.

Sweeney, Amin. *Malay Word Music: A Celebration of Oral Creativity*. Kuala Lumpur: Dewan Bahasa dan pustaka, Kementerian Pendidikan Malaysia, 1994.

Tanong do Kadazan/ Cerita Dongeng Kadazan/Kadazan Folk Tales. Pulou Tikus & I Lugodingon Om I Kookodu'. Sabah Folk Tales No. 3. Kota Kinabalu: Department of Sabah Museum and State Archives, 1990.

Taylor, Di. *Singapore Children's Favourite Stories*. Illustrated by L. K. Tay-Audouard. Singapore: Periplus, 2003.

Tersan, Reggie. *Myths and Legends from the Land of the Hornbill.* Subang Jaya, Selangor Darul Ehsan: Pelanduk Publications, 2001.

Tongo Tangon Kadazan Labuk-Kinabatangan/Cerita Dongeng Kadazan Labuk-Kinabatangan/Labuk-Kinabatangan Kadazan Folk Tales. Sabah Folk Tales. No. 1. Edited by Hope M. Hurlbut. Kota Kinabalu: Department of Sabah Museum, 1992.

Totunod Sungai/Tombonuwo/Cerita Dongeng Sungai/ Tombonuwo Sungai/Tombonuwo Folk Tales. Sabah Folk Tales No. 4. Compiled by John Wayne King and Julie K. King. Kota Kinabalu: Department of Sabah Museum and State Archives, 1990.

Velu, S. Kumara. *The Adventures of Sang Kancil, the Clever Mousedeer.* Kuala Lumpur: Tulur Pelita Sdn. Bhd., 1994.

Winstedt, Sir Richard. *A History of Classical Malay Literature.* Malaysian Branch of the Royal Asiatic Society. [1991?]. Revision of 1940, 1960 editions by Y. A. Taib.

GLOSSARY

Allah: one and only God

Anak: child

Anak-wagu: Kadazandusun word for young man

Ayam: chicken

Bangau: egret

Batu: rock

Bukit: hill

Burung: bird

Buwaya: crocodile

Carabao: water buffalo

Datu (Datuk): title of ruler

Dyak (Dayak): indigenous group of Borneo with more than 200 subgroups

Gadjah: elephant

Gasing: game played by spinning large wooden tops

Gergasi: monstrous giant

Gunong: mountain

Harimau: tiger

Iban: Dyak group of Borneo

Ikan: fish

Ikus: Kadazandusun word for mouse; the Malay word is *tikus*

Iman (Iman): religious leader

Jinn: magical spirit, genie

Johore: southernmost state in Peninsular Malaysia

Kambing: goat

Kampong (Kampung): small village

Kancil (Kantchil, Kantjil): mouse deer

Kenduri: feast

Kerbau: water buffalo

Kris: dagger; some are believed to possess magical powers

Majapahit: Hindu empire of the Malay archipelago circa 1293–1500

Malaka (Melaka, Malacca): city on western coast of Peninsular Malaysia

Malayou (Melayu): Malay

Minangkabau: indigenous group of Sumatera

Nasi: rice

Pak: honorific title

Palembang: city on eastern coast of Indonesian island of Sumatera

Pantun: poetic form used especially in courting and joking relationships

Parameswara: founder of the Melaka Kingdom

Penan: Dayak group of Borneo

Perak: state on northern part of western coast of Malaysia

Pirahu: canoe type boat

Pulau: island

Puteri: princess

Rajah: king, ruler

Sang: honorific title

Selamat pagi: good day

Shah: ruler

Singapura: Singapore

Sri: honorific title

Suleiman: Solomon

Sultan: king, ruler

Sumandak: Kadazandusun word for girl

Temasek: early name for Singapore

Tempayan: cooking pot

Tok: honorific title

Tolong: help!

Tun: honorific title

INDEX

Umbrella, royal, 26
Umbrella Hill, 51
Undersea travel, 15
Upstream, croc floats, 59

Vathanaprida, Supaporn, ix
Vegetables argue, 69–70
Vomit, eat, 17–18

Wai Wai, 164
Wan Darus, 37
War among vegetables, 69–70
Water
    is blood, 123
    proverb, 134
Water Buffalo, 75. *See also* Kerbau
Weather, proverb, 133
Wedding, dishes borrowed for, 51
Wee, Sheila, ix, xi, 11, 154, 169
West Indian Folk-Tales, 162
"White Crocodile, The," 103–105
    notes on, 164
White Rajah, 7
Whitman, Jen, x, 85, 105, 162–163
Whitman, Nat, x, 85, 105, 162–163

"Why Dog Is Treated Well," 108
    notes on, 166
Wife feeds giant, 79
Wild boar fails to rescue girl, 126
Windstedt, Richard, Sir, 158, 168
Wives of fools, 77
Wives unhappy with greedy husbands,
    110–111
Wonder Tales of Cats and Dogs, 155
Wood Beetle fails to fly over sea, 121
Wood shaving, 29
Woodpecker, 66
Word misconstrued, 76
World Folklore Series, ix
World War II, 5
Worm as child, 165

Xingu: The Indians and Their Myths, 164

Yahya, Raja Haji, 161
Yam
    brags, 69–70
    hides boy, 86–87
Yew, Lee Kuan, 6
YouTube, 149
Yunan, China, 166

ABOUT THE AUTHOR

MARGARET READ MACDONALD is an award-winning and internationally renowned author, storyteller, folklorist, and children's librarian. She has written or edited more than fifty books on storytelling and folklore topics. MacDonald travels extensively offering her "Playing with Story" workshops for teachers and librarians. Encouraging tellers met on her travels to contribute to the Libraries Unlimited World Folklore Series, MacDonald has edited five volumes for friends from Brazil, Cuba, Indonesia, Laos, and Thailand. She is currently at work on a collection with Saudi Arabian teller Nadia Taibah. For adults MacDonald has written *Ten Traditional Tellers* (2006).

Recent Titles in the
World Folklore Series

Princess Peacock: Tales from the Other Peoples of China
Retold by Haiwang Yuan

Lao Folktales
Kongdeuane Nettavong, Wajuppa Tossa; Edited by Margaret Read MacDonald

A Fire in My Heart: Kurdish Tales
Retold by Diane Edgecomb; with Contributions by Mohammed M.A. Ahmed and Çeto Ozel

The Flying Dutchman and Other Folktales from the Netherlands
Theo Meder

Folktales from the Japanese Countryside
As told by Hiroko Fujita; Edited by Fran Stallings with Harold Wright and Miki Sakurai

Mayan Folktales/Cuentos folklóricos mayas
Retold and Edited by Susan Conklin Thompson, Keith Thompson, and Lidia López de López

The Flower of Paradise and Other Armenian Tales
Translated and Retold by Bonnie C. Marshall; Edited and with a Foreword by Virginia Tashjian

The Magic Lotus Lantern and Other Tales from the Han Chinese
Haiwang Yuan

Brazilian Folktales
Livia de Almeida and Ana Portella; Edited by Margaret Read MacDonald

The Seven Swabians, and Other German Folktales
Anna Altmann

English Folktales
Edited by Dan Keding and Amy Douglas

The Snow Maiden and Other Russian Tales
Translated and Retold by Bonnie C. Marshall, Edited by Alla V. Kulagina

Additional titles in this series can be found at www.lu.com